Costume Reference 4

The Eighteenth Century

MARION SICHEL

B. T. Batsford Ltd, London

First published 1977
© Marion Sichel 1977
ISBN 0 7134 0340 3

Filmset by Servis Filmsetting Ltd,
Manchester

Printed in Great Britain by
The Anchor Press Ltd, Tiptree, Essex
for the Publishers B.T. Batsford Ltd,
4 Fitzhardinge Street, London W1H 0AH

Contents

Introduction

When we think of the clothes worn by our ancestors in the eighteenth century there is a temptation to see them as belonging to a unified style – a sort of fairly simple classical mode which corresponds to the period's concern with rationalism, balance and moderation. However, like most periods of history, when we look more closely at it we find many contradictions and divergences from the accepted pattern.

After all, not only are we dealing with four reigns: Anne (1702–14), George I (1714–27), George II (1727–60) and George III (1760–1820, although we shall only follow his reign in this volume to 1800) but also with some of the most radical changes in European and World history.

In fashion terms the first two reigns of the century made little impact on existing modes. The 'baroque' style was still dominant with its stiff and formal taste for high, cumbersome wigs for men and heavily brocaded materials for both male and female dress. Paris still effectively led costume taste and it was from here that innovations came, like the *contouche* or loose over-gown which established itself as the century progressed.

The unity between the ancient enemies – England and Scotland – which had been finally settled in the Act of Union of 1707 was very much under attack during the century. Not only in the form of two uprisings in Scotland in 1715 and 1745 but also from more profound changes. The old rural nature of society was changing in favour of increased industrialization which drew people away from their villages into the new cities like Birmingham, Manchester and Leeds. The more efficient methods of production changed the way people

Scottish dress with kilt, jacket and plaid, c.1745

dressed because now clothes manufacturers had machines which could standardize what had previously been done by hand: weaving, dyeing, spinning. With a new industrial labouring class to cater for and increasing means for the standardization of clothes making, the eighteenth century heralded the birth of mass-production – a revolution which now dominates our own fashion scene.

Periwig with falling curls tied with ribbon, c.1761

6

Two other great hammer-blows to traditional British society made their impact on dress: the loss of the American colonies in 1776 and the French Revolution of 1789. Before these events fashionable costume was led by artistocratic France and the modes display the taste of their aristocratic wearers: elegant but not functional (often panniered skirts could have wire frames supporting them six metres wide), wigs were elaborate piles which owed more to the engineer's craft than the couturier's art, delicate silks were favoured in pale pastel colours often decorated with bird or flower motifs (these designs were part of the fashionable rage for all things Chinese whether in costume, painting, furniture, wallpapers and upholstery).

The growth of a prosperous middle class through industrialization and foreign trade, the impact of mechanized manufacture on clothing, the ideas of democracy unleashed by the American and French Revolutions and, interestingly, the passion for ancient Greek or Roman styles which grew rapidly as the century advanced, all served to undermine the aristocratic style we call 'rococo'. In its place was a new ideal of simplicity, unostentatious dress and a measure of functionality best seen in the increasing use by men of dark suits made of serviceable materials and in children's costume which, perhaps for the first time, ceased to be merely a replica of their parents and strove to give them more freedom of movement.

Male Costume

Men's clothes remained fairly constant in their essential appearance, the changes mainly being in the cut. Materials also varied, plainer ones being used for everyday wear, and brocades, silks and great ornamentation for dress or Court wear. Double-breasted coats were worn mainly by the lower classes, although they could be worn for riding, or sometimes by the military. Basically a suit consisted of a coat or frock, waistcoat and breeches.

COATS 1700–50

Coats varied in length and were close fitting and waisted. The skirt which was fully flared had three vents to hip level, one either side and one centre back. The side seams came straight down from the armholes. The side vents had five or six pleats which after *c.*1720 were reduced to only three or four. *Hip-buttons* which were covered in the same material as the coat were used as decoration at the top of the vents to where the pleats were stitched. Occasionally one or two buttons were sewn inside the pleats beneath the vents, almost closing the vent but allowing enough gap for a sword to be worn. These pleated vents were often stiffened with buckram so as to flare out from the waist when the coat was closed in front. The single vent at the back was, from the beginning of the century until the 1730s, without a pleat although an inverted pleat became popular from then until the 1770s.

The coat was collarless and, until the 1720s, low cut in front, gradually rising so as to fit around the neck.

The front hung straight, but overlapped slightly when closed. From the end of the 1730s the front edges were made

Coat with closed slit sleeves and vertical pockets, c.1718–20

8

Coat with round cuffs and waistcoat, c.1764

to curve back slightly, so the side seams (which had been straight down until the 1720s) also curved back, thereby bringing the hip-buttons closer together at the back. This trend continued until the end of the century. Coats were buttoned from neck to hem, but when the fronts began to be curved back buttoning reached to just beneath waist level.

Buttonholes were made long, but sewn together leaving just enough open for a button to pass through. Occasionally sham buttonholes were also placed on the opposite side with the buttons. Buttonholes on the buttonhole side were very often also sham except for a few at the waist when it was fashionable to have a frilled shirt visible in the front, so that the coat was only closed at waist level.

Hooks-and-eyes were also used as a form of fastening, especially for coats that were ornate and heavily embroidered. Sometimes a top button at the neck was also closed.

Pockets which lay horizontally had oblong flaps which were rounded until *c.*1710 and then vertical pockets were popular (only up to the first decade of the century) with openings covered by narrow flaps with decorative buttons. There were no inside pockets on the coats until the second half of the century. Coats with vertical pockets usually had sleeves without cuffs known as *slit sleeves*. These were close-fitting to the wrist with a vertical slit on the outside seam. These could be buttoned, but were mainly left open to reveal shirt sleeves and ruffles. The suit sleeve could be turned back to resemble a small cuff. Originally sleeves were loose-fitting, wider at the wrists, but became close-fitting after *c.*1710.

Cuffed sleeves ended wrist level to allow the shirt sleeve to be visible. *Open cuffs*, also known as *open sleeves* were quite deep from about 1710, becoming deeper about 1727 and very deep by the 1730s. The wings of the cuffs curved round to the back up to elbow height and were often attached to the sleeve with decorative buttons at the end, the buttonholes sometimes being false and the cuff sewn on. Cuffs became lower in the 1740s and fell away from the sleeve at the back. By mid-century, however, this style had become unfashionable. Round *closed cuffs* had been popular throughout the period and were (apart frrom a slit) similar to the open cuff, and in the 1730s they curved around the elbows and were extremely deep. They were known as *boot cuffs* or *boot sleeves*.

FROCK COATS 1700–50

A *frock* before 1730 was a loose type of coat with a flat turned-down collar worn mainly by the working classes to guard the outer clothes from dirt (the corresponding attire for countrymen was the smock). The frock was worn by the upper classes for riding. It was cut in a similar fashion to the coat, but more flexible and therefore easy to wear. The main variation was in the neckline and sleeves. The flat, turned-down collar, known as a 'cape' was occasionally lined in a contrasting colour. The sleeves reached wrist level with a round closed cuff which was wide and deep until about 1750; a shorter sleeve without cuffs was also quite popular. Fastening was by buttons, usually of metal, down the front.

COATS 1750–1800

Men's coats remained essentially the same as for the first half of the century. The side seams of the close-fitting coats began to curve back so that the back became narrower and the top buttons closer together. At the same time the fronts were also curved back so that the breeches were more visible. By the 1760s the flared skirt became extinct and by the 1790s square coat-tails, ending above knee level at the back were all that remained. The stiffening of skirts fell into disuse in the 1760s, and from the 1780s the chest part of the coat was beginning to be padded.

Side vents consisted of three pleats and hip-buttons. The pleats were usually caught at the buttons which could be down the sides, and almost hidden by the pleats. The back vent had folds either side until about 1775 and was trimmed with sham buttonholes which were very popular from about 1760.

Until *c.*1765 these coats had been collarless but from that date a *standing collar* was worn, about $2\frac{1}{2}$ cm high, increasing to 4 cm and higher in the 1790s. Sometimes this collar had a small step under the chin.

The curving away of the fronts of the coat from the waist down became very marked from the 1770s, and by the 1790s hardly any skirts remained in the front.

Buttons were mainly fastened at the waist only, although there were buttons from neck-to-waist, and occasionally even down to the hemline. During this later period buttons were no longer domed but flat. They were medium size until about 1775, and then became quite large. The really big

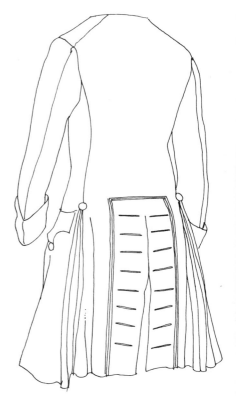

Silk coat with full, stiffened side pleats, c.1760–70

buttons, popular until *c*.1788, were used mainly for frocks and undress wear.

Buttonholes, although in general very long, were usually sewn up leaving just enough opening for a button to pass through. Sham buttonholes were very popular and were sometimes on both sides of an opening as decoration. They sloped upwards from the edges. This was because of the curvature of the fronts. If all the buttonholes were sham, fastening was by means of hooks-and-eyes, which gave an edge to edge closure.

Military coats had long, narrow revers from the neck to almost waist level which were fastened back with buttons – a style sometimes also worn by civilians.

Pockets were placed each side of the coat just below the waist with flaps less deep, but the sham buttonholes remained with buttons placed beneath, on the coat. From the 1780s, pocket-holes usually had welts, sham pockets with just flaps becoming less general. *Slit pockets* which were placed vertically just before the side vents were without flaps and were often worn by people who carried the tools of their trade in their pockets.

Sleeves which allowed the ruffled shirt sleeves to be seen were fairly close-fitting with puckering at the shoulders from the 1790s. *Cuffs* were generally worn in various styles, closed all round. They could be quite wide with wings (in the 1750s) and during the 1760s and 1770s they were closed, deep or small. A small close-fitting cuff known as *à la marinière* (naval fashion), was worn from about 1750. This was crossed in the front with a scalloped flap with three or four matching buttons of which the bottom ones could be left open. In the 1790s sham cuffs which were just a row of stitching could also be worn. Wide, open cuffs which had been popular, become outmoded in the 1760s.

WAISTCOATS 1700–50

A *waistcoat*, similar to the coat in cut, was close-fitting to the waist with buckram-stiffened skirts and unpleated vents. The flared skirt was always shorter than the coat and usually reached to above knee level. After 1740 the back was slightly shorter than the front. For sport the younger generation wore very short waistcoats with hardly any skirt at all. The front skirts sloped out from the tops of the side vents, making the base wider at an acute angle at the hem. The back vent could

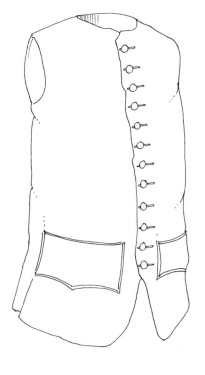

Satin waistcoat, c.1760–70

Gentleman wearing a bag wig
with a large bow at the back and
a large bow in the front. The
lady is wearing a mantua with
the train folded into the back
draping, c.1730

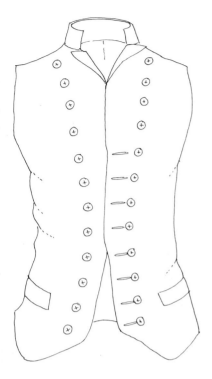

Sleeveless double-breasted waistcoat, c.1780

Short double-breasted waistcoat with square-cut hem, and narrow standing collar, c.1780

be open to shoulder height and laced to the owner's fit, or tapes could be used and tied.

The parts of the waistcoat not visible beneath the coat were often made of a cheaper material than the rest. This was usually the back of the vents and the sleeves to elbow level. The waistcoat was collarless and like the coat in this early period was curved away at the front, making more of the breeches visible.

The waistcoat was fastened with buttons, smaller than but matching those of the coat. They extended from neck to hem from 1700–60, although they became less popular after about 1740. The buttons were seldom closed below the waist. If the waistcoat had edge to edge fastening, it was by means of hooks-and-eyes. This method was usually only used on heavily embroidered waistcoats.

From the 1730s the waistcoat could be double-breasted, the left front over the right, with the buttons close together at waist level, but further apart above. Lapels, when present, were formed by the edges of the waistcoat being turned back.

WAISTCOATS 1750–1800

Pockets were similar, but not as large as coat pockets, and were usually placed horizontally, with flaps.

Waistcoats had sleeves (until 1760) which were close-fitting, without cuffs and often extended below the coat sleeves. They had a slit at the wrist, and although a button and buttonhole were present, this was usually left undone. Sleeved waistcoats were worn by servants until the end of the century as jackets, usually without a coat. When intended for indoor wear and to be worn without a coat, they usually had the back and sleeves of the same material as the rest.

The waistcoat which, by 1760, was now sleeveless, had the front skirts shorter and cut back, thus making the angle of the overlap sharper. In the 1780s side vents went out of fashion and the front skirts became just flaps. When, in the 1790s, square waistcoats became fashionable, the acute-angled style went out of fashion.

Single-breasted waistcoats were usually only fastened at the waist, although buttons reached from the neck to the curved-away part below the waistline. This curve increased from the 1760s. From *c.*1770 small lapels were added to the collarless waistcoat which could have a V-shaped front.

Double-breasted waistcoats were often buttoned with one to four buttons with the wide overlap on the right side buttoned up to a large lapel, whilst the other was hidden beneath. This style was popular in the 1760s, and on rare occasions they were without skirts for riding. This would leave the waistcoat with a straight base. Double-breasted waistcoats were worn less in the 1770s, but again were common in the 1780s with longer skirts and low standing collars with lapels. A style characteristic of the 1760s, was a waistcoat with buttoning at the waist, above which a side overlap was buttoned up forming the lapel on the right side, whilst the left lapel was tucked in. The usual double-breasted waistcoat of the 1780s had two rows of buttons, closely placed, spreading outwards towards the shoulders after the top buttonhole. A standing collar was worn with this style, either narrow or wide. The lapels were formed in a point making a V-shape opening at the neck. The bottom of the waistcoat could be either square cut or a wide cut-away. Very popular in this period were stripes, either vertical or horizontal, and also sometimes a white silk fringe edged the lapels and front edge.

During the 1790s, when the waistcoat was square cut, the two rows of buttons were placed wider apart, and as the waistcoat was now shorter, there were fewer of them.

The neckline with its standing collar generally had deep angular lapels which could be turned over those of the double-breasted coat. Another style of collar, a shawl type, was low and turned down in one with the lapels and was without a step.

Also in the 1790s *under-waistcoats* began to be worn. These were made to be seen, and mainly had shawl collars, although occasionally standing collars could also be worn which appeared over the turned-back lapels of the over-waistcoats. The under-waistcoat was invariably shorter than the over type and was square cut, closed with only two or three buttons with the visible part made of a brighter and better-quality material than the rest. Under-waistcoats (worn for warmth and known as *camisoles*) were usually made of flannel or other warm material and were worn as an undergarment with sleeves.

Waistcoat buttons, smaller than coat buttons, were matched to the coat when worn as a suit. Waistcoat pockets, of which there were usually two, had flaps similar to those of the coat flaps, being rectangular in the 1770s; the welted pockets being without flaps from the 1780s and used on square-cut or double-breasted waistcoats. Sometimes, when there were no pockets, flaps would be placed over sham ones.

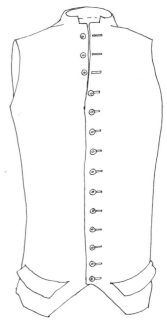

Silk waistcoat, c.1775–85

Satin waistcoat, coat and breeches, c.1770–80

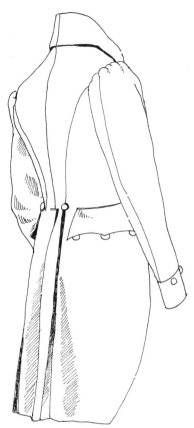

Single-breasted coat with high turned-down collar, c. 1785–95

The *back*, usually shorter than the front parts, had a deep vent at the centre from about 1765–70, after which the vent became shorter (square-cut waistcoats had no vent). It was usually made of a cheaper material as the back was not seen, although the skirts each side of the back vent were made of the better material. This idea became very popular from the 1780s. To give a better fit to the waistcoat, the back was often tightened with either tapes or ribbons.

Waistcoats were sleeveless in the 1750s except for older men who preferred sleeves. In the 1790s when sleeves were again worn for a brief time, they were gathered at the shoulder seam, similar to the coat sleeve.

FROCK COATS 1750–1800

The *frock* was worn with a turned-down collar (1750–70) for undress and sport, after which date it could be worn on all occasions, except at Court. It was known as a frock coat when worn in place of a coat and cut in an elegant style. The *English frock* was plain, trimmed with braid or frogging, whilst the *French frock* which could be worn at Court was more elaborately embellished with embroidery. It was often shorter than the coat and, when worn on sporting occasions, the skirts were turned back for comfort.

Collars varied from being flat or rolled in the 1760s, becoming narrow for a brief while in the 1770s, to those falling away in short squared flaps either side. In the 1780s, a popular style emerged which rose at the back with a turnover coming to a slight point in the front. A turned-down collar, similar to a cape, was often faced with a contrasting coloured material. On elegant occasions from *c.*1785, a stand-fall type of collar became usual wear.

Frock fastening was by means of buttons which could come to below waist level. The skirts curved away from the front and the back became narrower so that by the 1790s they had become coat-tails.

The frock was normally single-breasted and without lapels until about 1780, after which lapels became more common with the double-breasted style. These lapels were usually small, and a button was often placed between it and the collar. The front buttons were placed fairly close together, whilst in the 1790s lapels became wider and sometimes rounded. After about 1796 the gap between lapel and collar was quite large and the front buttoning became further apart.

Buttons were usually made of metal, gold or silver, and

after 1770 (when buttons became larger) of steel or mother-of-pearl. They were at their largest by 1777. Buttons with enamelled designs became popular from 1770. Buttonholes, however, were mainly quite plain.

Pockets, similar to coat pockets, had plain flaps without sham buttonholes and buttons after the 1780s. Pockets inside the lining became popular from *c.*1777, and could be used with or without outside pockets.

After 1770 *sleeves* became more close-fitting having had round cuffs in the 1750s which became narrower and deeper in the 1760s. It was common to have a row of three buttons at the upper edge.

Cuffs à la marinière were also still in common use, but the most popular type from about 1780 was with a short vertical slit at the wrist and a vertical flap which could be left partially open.

NECKWEAR

Cravats were popular until the 1740s although still worn by the elderly after that date. They were made of a band of material such as linen or lawn, and tied loosely beneath the chin with ends either lace edged or decorated with tasselled beads. Another method of wearing a cravat, known as a 'Steinkirk', was with the front ends twisted and the terminals either passed through a buttonhole or attached with a brooch to one side of the coat. The popularity of this style remained with the older generation until the 1770s, although it had become generally unfashionable as early as the 1730s.

From *c.*1735 a high neckband called a *stock* which could be stiffened and usually made of lawn or cambric became popular. This allowed the ruffled shirt to be seen in the front. Those gallants of high fashion, the 'Macaronis' favoured a necktie (a strip of material with either lace or tasselled ends). The stock was folded and worn around the neck with a buckle closure either at the front or back. It gradually increased in height and was stiffened with pasteboard making it extremely uncomfortable. The buckles used, although often hidden by the wig, were usually of precious metals, occasionally studded with diamonds.

The *solitaire,* worn until the 1770s (mainly with a bag wig) was a black tie worn over a stock. This was a broad black ribbon worn around the neck with the ends at the front being either tied, left to dangle, or else pinned to the front.

For recreation or informal occasions neckwear was not

Coat and waistcoat of the period 1780–90

(Right)
On the left a peasant farm worker of the period. The lady is wearing a wrapping gown over a dome-shaped hoop petticoat, the bodice cut 'en fourreau' with the skirt, worn here without a modesty piece. The gentleman has both waistcoat and coat fastenings from neck to hem with buttons, and is wearing a long full-bottomed wig, c.1720.

16

always worn. In that case the shirt was left open at the neck and the waistcoat normally worn closed.

The working classes often only wore a folded neckerchief, if anything, around the neck.

BREECHES 1700–50

Knee breeches were worn by all classes throughout the eighteenth century. The typical style had a very wide angle at the crotch. The seat of the breeches was ample and shapeless, the top being gathered on to a waistband. The legs, wide at the top, narrowed to just below the knees and terminated with a kneeband. The lower part of the outer seam was closed with three or four buttons and buttonholes.

Gartered stockings were pulled over the breeches to over the knees until about mid-century. These stockings, known as 'roll-ups', were turned down into a flat roll over the garters. From *c*.1735 the kneeband below the knee was sometimes closed with a buckle fastening over the stockings. These buckles, which were quite small in the first half of the century, often matched those of the shoes.

Breeches buttoned in the front,
c.1740

The waistband was deeper in the front and closed with buttons, but at the back, a small slit was closed by lacing so as to tighten and make the breeches fit. This was often done at hip level. After *c*.1745 a strap and buckle replaced the lacing at the back. Breeches were closed by two methods. Up until the 1750s they could be buttoned down the front with the buttons on the right and a strip of material with buttonholes sewn to the left side of the fly opening. The buttons were usually covered in the same material as the breeches. These breeches could have pockets with flaps at the front at thigh level which were horizontally placed and were closed with a button on a corner flap to the waistband. Vertical pockets were sometimes in the side seams on either side, although there was often only one pocket on the right side. There could also be a small pocket in the waistband on each side. The other method of fastening the breeches was with a drop-down flap known as a 'fall'. This style was popular from *c*.1730 onwards. A 'small fall' was a flap in the centre front of the breeches to cover the opening and this was fastened by buttons to the waistband. A 'whole fall' was a larger flap which reached the side seams and was closed with buttons on either side and one at the top centre on the waistband.

Breeches with a small fall
closure, c.1740

BREECHES 1750–1800

Breeches became more close fitting in the second half of the eighteenth century but were still made in the same way. In the 1750s they were shorter, exposing the knees, rolled up stockings no longer reaching them. From the early 1780s they became known as 'small clothes'. Ornamental ribbon garters

Short-bodied breeches, c.1764

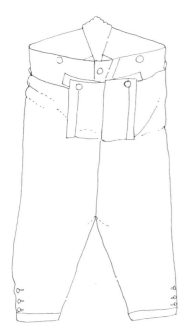

Breeches with long body and legs, with single brace buttons, c.1786

Slightly long-waisted double-breasted dressing gown, c.1770–80

could be worn for show with the knee buckles small and square.

In the 1760s when breeches were longer and again worn over the knees, the buckles were square and came in a variety of sizes. Towards 1778, the 'Macaronis' popularized ribbon ties which could be worn instead of buckles, and embroidered knee bands came into fashion from about 1787.

In the 1780s tight fitting breeches became long in the body and legs with brace buttons either side at the front beginning to make their appearance, and buttons at knee level at either side. Knee buckles, which were large and oval but seldom round, were worn vertically so that the knee bands had a slight dip to accommodate them.

Pantaloons – a type of close fitting tights ending at the ankles – were worn from the 1790s. They were buttoned up the legs in the outside up to the calf, and pulled tight around the ankle with a running string. The method of closure at the top was of the fall type.

Braces, called 'gallowses', were generally worn after 1787 and became increasingly important as the breeches were no longer so tight fitting at the waist, and therefore needed to be held up.

INDOOR WEAR

Indoor garments became very popular during the early part of the eighteenth century. Usually worn around the house as a negligée was a *banjan* which was a loose type of dressing gown to about knee level. The back had a short vent and the front was of the wrap-over kind, fastening with either clasps, hooks-and-eyes or buttons. The sleeves were usually close-fitting and slit at the wrists. During the 1780s the banjan also became popular as outdoor wear.

Another style of *morning gown* was long and loose, with a wrap-over front tied with a sash at the waist, and sometimes made with a roll collar. The long loose sleeves were often rolled back at the wrists. These garments were usually worn with nightcaps.

The *negligée* or nightgown, or morning gown as it was also known, did not alter much this century, still being a loose garment usually tied around the waist with either a girdle or the front just being wrapped over. These gowns, never worn as night attire, were worn for comfort indoors instead of a frock or a coat.

OUTDOOR WEAR 1700–50

For outdoor wear a *greatcoat* or *surtout* was worn. This was usually came below knee level and was loose fitting. Cut in four parts it was seamed beneath the arms and had a seam down the centre back, but was without a waist seam. The flared skirt was not as pleated as a coat, and the side vents were optional, except that a slit on the left side was essential for the sword to protrude. A back vent was also necessary as these surtouts were often worn when riding.

A surtout usually had two collars, a larger flat one similar to a cape, and over this a smaller one which could be pulled up and buttoned at the front during inclement weather. If the smaller collar was absent, a narrow upright band would be attached instead. Fastening was by means of buttoning, although usually only closed to waist level from the neck. Belts of the same materials were often buttoned in front. They were either complete belts or just half belts coming from the side seams. The wide sleeves ended in round cuffs which could be decorated with buttons and buttonholes.

Cloaks, which remained popular until the 1750s, were full and long. They were gathered at the neck and fastened with a clasp. When worn for riding a deep back vent was necessary.

Another type of cloak, known as the *Roquelaure*, was shorter, usually only to the knees, and with a vent at the back when worn for riding. It was not gathered at the neck, but was cut in four pieces and shaped to flare out. It could either have one or two collars and closure was by buttoning down the front.

OUTDOOR WEAR 1750–1800

In the second half of the century for outdoor wear the *surtout*, a large and loose overcoat, was worn. This followed the shape of the frock, although the front skirts were not sloped. By the 1780s it was fashionable to wear the surtout well below knee length. The collar, cape-like, consisted of two or three falling capes of different and overlapping lengths, the top one close to the neck, often with velvet facings.

Double-breasted greatcoats had lapels, unlike their single-breasted cousins. Fastening was by large metal buttons to just below waist level. The sleeves were full and had round cuffs with buttons around the top border. The pockets had flaps and were placed rather far back; vertical pockets being less frequently used.

Redingote greatcoat often with two or three collars, c.1786

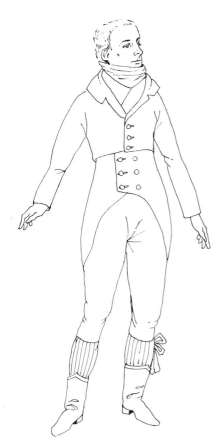

Short spencer worn over jacket. Breeches are long with short Hessian-type boots, c.1795

After about 1750 cloaks were mainly worn by professional people, the army and for funerals. The *spencer*, a coat without tails, ending at the waist like a jacket, was closed with buttons down the front. The long sleeves ended in cuffs, and the neckline had a stand-fall collar. This type of jacket, worn from the 1790s, was worn outdoors over the frock or coat.

FOOTWEAR 1700–50

Both men and women wore *buckled shoes* similar to the previous century, except that the designs were more delicate. The tabs became higher, the buckles more elegant and the heels more shaped. Red heels, still popular, were mainly worn for Court or formal occasions. Most heels were made of either leather, wood or cork, Deep, squared toes again became fashionable with corresponding square high heels. Tall square tongues which complimented the rest of the shoes were lined in contrasting colours. Scalloped tongues were fashionable until *c.*1716. The sides of the shoes were closed, and were fastened with straps and large buckles over a tall tongue. As shoes became less square shaped (about 1750) heels and tongues became lower and smaller.

In the beginning of the century *buckles* were small, but became larger after 1740. The small buckles were either oblong or square shaped, becoming larger from *c.* 1725. They were made mainly of metal and could be decorated with jewels.

For riding, *jackboots* or half-jackboots to just below the knees were worn. The heavy jackboots had squared, blocked toes with the squared heels to match. By the 1740s the squareness became less obvious. The boots had large bucket tops and were worn with broad spur leathers and star-shaped rowels. The lighter jackboot was more shaped to the leg, over the knee with a dip at the back to allow for easy movement.

Pumps were mainly worn by the fashionable and were low-heeled shoes with a thin, supple sole; they were fastened with a buckle over the tongue.

Gaiters were worn shaped to the leg with foot extensions and reached to above knee level. Also called *spatterdashes* they were fastened by either lacing or buttons on the outside edge with a buckle strap under the instep to hold them to the feet. They were mainly worn by the military, but also by civilians for riding in place of boots. Countrymen wore a shorter form of spatterdash, reaching to calf length only.

21

STOCKINGS 1700–50

Stockings were worn over the breeches above the knees and then rolled over garters which fastened beneath the knees and under the stockings. These were popular until the 1750s. *Long stockings* to above knee level were usually knitted either by hand or machine. The clocks were often knitted in a design or embroidered in a variety of colours. They were made of either cottons, wools or silk and were in many differing colours. *Garters* were made of strips of woven silk, sometimes with designs or chequered. Thicker stockings were worn inside jackboots over thinner stockings as protection.

FOOTWEAR 1750–1800

By 1750 the rounded and squared toes had again become more pointed, although the rounded type were still worn.

Smart overshoes known as *clogs* were made to match shoes so that they looked as one. Wooden-soled *pattens* with metal rings (used from the second half of the seventeenth century right through to the Victorian period) were worn mainly by the poorer classes.

Heels were generally lower by the 1760s and had become quite flat by the 1790s. Red heels were worn for Court wear, except for a short period between 1760–70. *Slippers*, a type of mule, were mainly made of Moroccan leather and were highly decorative.

Hussar boots, also known as *Hessian boots*, from the soldiers of the German principality of Hess, were popular at the end of the century. They were a type of short riding boot, close fitting to just below the knee, slightly higher in the front which was often decorated with a tassel. They were mainly in black with a coloured border on top.

Other fashionable boots were again being worn and one style of great popularity was the *top boot* or *jockey boot* with the top turned down. This was usually made of a grained leather with the inside brown and the outside black. The turned-back cuff was often made in a white chamois leather.

Seamless boots made from animal's legs were fashionable, but seams could also be hidden on the cheaper variety by a special paste whilst egg white and lamp soot were used as polish.

Highlows, boots which came up to the calf and laced in front, were worn mainly by country people and the working classes from *c*.1785.

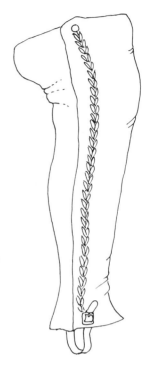

Long spatterdash

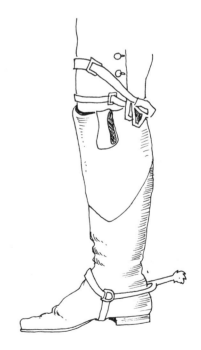

English jockey top boot

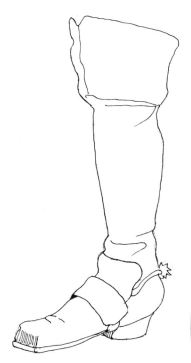

Heavy jackboot with the squared blocked toes, c.1720

Hair powder puffer, c.1770

STOCKINGS 1750–1800

Vertically striped stockings were very popular in the 1780s and 1790s with black and white, or blue and white the most fashionable colours. By 1790 zig-zag patterns were also favoured.

Garters with designs woven in were usually placed twice around the legs and tied below knee level. The knee-band of the breeches could cover them and leave the tasselled ends hanging on the outer side of the leg.

WIGS 1700–50

Wigs originated in France and reached England in the Restoration (see *Costume Reference 3*) and became so large in the eighteenth century that for comfort they were removed when indoors, and nightcaps were worn instead. Some kind of head attire was essential as the head was mainly shaven or cut very short like the modern 'crew-cut'.

Wheat-powder was first used for powdering the wig, and pure white powder was introduced early in the century (c.1703). Powder could also be made of earth and a combination of plaster of paris and starch. Although the usual colours were grey or white, the dandies favoured colours like blue, brown, pink, black, all which were perfumed. Before the powder was applied the hair was greased to make it adhere and a hand bellow was used by a servant to spray the powder on to the wig, the face being covered over during this extraordinary operation. The fashion for powdered wigs lasted almost 100 years, until the French Revolutionary period and after a tax had been levied from 1795.

To make the curls on wigs special clay pipes in a variety of sizes, were used. These were heated and used in the same way as modern curling tongs. Natural hair was curled with paper.

There was an abundance of wig styles. The *full bottomed* wig with the front hair in peaks either side of the parting continued in fashion from the previous century, but after about 1730 this became smaller and less popular, being worn mainly by older or professional men. The full-bottomed wig had a mass of curls framing the face and then falling to below shoulder level. After c.1710, the peaks became lower, and after c.1720, the locks also became shorter, and hung chiefly behind.

From 1700 wigs with *queues* (pig-tails) were fashionable. They became popular mainly for convenience as the masses of hair were more comfortable and manageable if tied back.

Pig-tail wig, c. 1790

A style, known as the *tie wig* was popular from *c.*1710. This had the curls at the back held together with a black ribbon bow at the nape of the neck. Another variation, known as the *pigtail wig* and worn informally could have the plait at the back interlaced with a black ribbon and bound in a spiral, and another fashionable mode, the *bag wig*, had the hair at the back in a stiff black bag tied with drawstrings at the nape of the neck and finished in a large bow.

The *scratch bob* was usually in the colour of the hair of the wearer, the natural hair being brushed back from the forehead to blend in with the wig and fixed with *pomatum* (a perfumed hair-oil). The *physical wig*, which replaced the full-bottomed wig from the 1750s for professional men, was similar to a long bob, being brushed back from the front without a parting. *Campaign wigs* worn until the 1750s had a centre parting with wavy or curled hair on either side, with a long curl hanging down tied into a knot, whilst the back hair fell in a single curl to the nape of the neck.

Wigs with queues became smaller in the second half of the century and curls were worn less. The rolls of curls were hollow and stiff and were known as buckles from the French word *boucle* (curl). Up to *c.*1750 side hair was worn in bunches over the ears in a style known as *pigeon's wings*.

The *toupée*, fashionable in the 1750s and 1760s, had the front hair brushed straight back with two horizontal curls just above ear level on either side and in the late 1760s and 1770s the front hair was raised on pads. The toupée could become egg-shaped or fanned out on top, but came straight down without sloping to the back of the head. The version which had a curl around the head just above the ears was known as *staring wings* and was worn with a pigtail wig.

The *Ramillies wig* (after the battle of Ramillies in 1706) was principally a military fashion. It consisted of a back in one or more plaits with a large bow worn at the nape of the neck and a smaller one at the end of the plait. Popular throughout the century it changed little until the 1780s when the plait was often turned up and fastened with a comb to the back of the wig, or tied with a ribbon up to the nape of the neck. From 1780–1800 very often a simple roll curl from one side of the head over the front to the other side was worn, with a queue at the back.

A *catagon* or *club wig*, which was worn from the 1760s, was wide and flat, and turned up and tied around the centre. The colourful Macaronis wore large versions of these.

Tie wig, c.1750–60

LEFT: *c.*1725. Black tricorne laced in gold, decorated with bows and feathers. Full natural coloured wig. The coat was decorated with gold lace. The high knee boots were favoured by the military.

CENTRE: *c.*1745. A Scottish costume depicts a gentleman wearing a belted plaid.

RIGHT: *c.*1735. Typical street tradesman dressed in the fashion of the day, jacket and breeches. Wearing a large uncocked hat and tied around the waist was a large white apron.

TOP LEFT: *c.*1760. Tight sleeves with treble flounces, a handkerchie[f] over the shoulders and a muslin apron. A bergère hat worn over an undercap.

RIGHT: *c.*1770. Open robe à la Française with a stomacher. Sleeves ending just above the elbows revealing ruffles of lace.

BOTTOM LEFT: *c.*1776. Little girl wearing a smaller version of a grow[n] up dress with short sleeves and a round décolletage.

There was also a military wig, worn by civilians and soldiers from the 1750s, similar to a bob wig, with two long curls tied at the nape of the neck and left to hang down, forming a double queue. After *c.* 1775 the long queue was often looped-up and held to the head by a small comb.

The *Cadogan wig*, popular from about 1770, had the back hair looped and tied in the centre. And, again, a large version of this style was very popular with the Macaronis.

Another popular style from *c.*1780, similar to the female style, *à la herisson* or *hedgehog*, had the top and sides brushed out into spikes.

Physical wig, c.1755–56

Full toupée with ends in curls, c.1789

Toupée with side curls, c.1780

Campaign wig which shows the knot in the lock of hair, c.1741

Ramillies wig with queue tied up, c.1780

Catogan or club wig, c.1770

*Wig with catogan queue and
a fantail hat, c.1786*

*Full-bottomed wig showing the
long fall down the chest and the
other side falling to the shoulder,
c.1715–20*

*High hair style worn by the
Macaronis, c.1774*

*Hedgehog or natural hairstyle,
c.1785*

Nightcap, c.1785

HAIRSTYLES

During the 1790s the men had their own hair cut short into a variety of styles, from a short crop to shoulder- or chin-length hair.

The *Brutus crop*, a windswept style, was worn by both male and females.

HEADWEAR 1700–50

Hats were less popular in the eighteenth century due to the extensive use of wigs. However, there were various styles, many of which were meant only to be carried (for example the *chapeau bras* styles, so popular in the 1770s).

A *three-cornered hat*, known later in the nineteenth century as a 'tricorne', had a brim turned up on three sides, thus forming a triangular shape. One of the points always faced front. The brim could be bound in braid or feather edged. For formal wear a button and loop was often worn on the left cock, or turned up brim. The *Kevenhuller hat* was a variation of this basic shape and had the front peak pinched or dented in.

Small *cocked hats* were popular in the 1730s, whilst larger ones, like the *Dettingen cock*, named after the battle of Dettingen in 1743, were slightly taller variations. Although it was fashionable to carry these hats under the arm, the *chapeau bras* made specifically for this fashion, only became fashionable in the 1770s.

A round crowned hat with a rigid brim was worn by professional men, whilst the soft brim was more popular amongst the younger and middle classes. Whilst beaver was the most popular material for hats, straw could be used for the round hats. And, for riding, jockey caps were popular. They were round and had flat peaks in the front and were always in black.

For indoor wear, when wigs were removed, soft caps were worn. These were usually round crowned with flat turned-up brims. The crown could be quite tall and have a large bow. Another style was a shapeless, floppy crown from which sometimes hung a tassel and a rolled brim. Plain caps were worn in bed and were usually made of lined or quilted cotton.

HEADWEAR 1750–1800

The *military hat* was broad brimmed with a turned back brim near the crown and was decorated with a cockade – a style also popular with the younger aristocrats. The *sailor's*

A beaver round hat, c. 1790

High standing fall-collar coat with round cuffs. Bicorne hat with a cockade, c. 1788

cock was similar, the brim which formed an equilateral triangle was joined to the crown. Macaronis often wore a small version of the three-cornered hat which could be trimmed with a feather.

The *fantail hat* of the 1780s was so called because the brim at the back was half-round, and stood upright like a fan. The front part of the brim stood up and sloped down each side to allow only the flat-topped crown to be visible at the gaps at the sides. It could be decorated with a button loop on the left, but if worn by the military had a cockade or feather.

The *chapeau bras* carried under the arm from the 1770s was an even triangular brimmed flat hat. The brim could be fastened to the crown and a feather used for decoration. Opera hats were similar.

Another variation of the three-cornered hat was the *Nivernois hat* which had a low round crown and very wide brim turned over at the edges to form a large triangle. The peak was worn in front. This hat was often worn for protection against rain. *Quaker hats* were similar, with the exception of a taller crown.

A *bicorne*, worn from the 1780s, had the brim turned up at the front and back with the crown completely hidden. The brim was pressed in at the front to form a peak, and was usually decorated on the left with either a cockade or rosette. This type of hat could be worn for riding and was sometimes decorated with a hatband and buckle in the front.

ACCESSORIES

Gloves, in contrast to the seventeenth century (see *Costume Reference 3*), were quite simple and made mainly of leather and wool. If they were short they ended at the wrists with a short slit at the back or, alternatively, they could have small turned-back cuffs which were sometimes embroidered. Longer gloves were worn until about 1730 and reached above the wrists also with a slit at the back and sometimes edged with a fringe. *Mittens* were popular too and usually had one compartment for the fingers and one for the thumb. The mitten cuffs, which could be plain, could also be leather-lined. *Muffs* both large and small were in fashion until the 1730s and then until the 1750s became extremely large. They were worn attached to a cord or ribbon worn around the neck, or could be looped to a coat button, or hung from the waistbelt. Worn on all occasions fashionable young gentlemen preferred them scented. They were made of a variety of

Nightwatchman in a greatcoat,
c.1770

materials such as feathers and furs, often ribbon trimmed. From the 1740s small *wrist muffs* were worn for both warmth and for protection of the complicated shirt wrist-ruffles.

Swords were carried until the 1780s, and from then on only for ceremonial occasions. From *c.*1730 the sword was superseded by a cane and for a while both were in use. A sword belt was worn under the waistcoat, and from the frog (a kind of button and loop) hung the sword. The hilt, which was of precious metals and could be ornamented with jewels, protruded from the side vent of the coat on the left side. Attached to the hilt was a sword knot, usually made of bunches of ribbon.

Canes, which began to come into fashion early in the century, could be either long or short with a very ornate head sometimes beautifully carved, either made of a precious metal or stones, like amber. These heads were detachable and in the hollow, scent or other things could be carried. *Sticks* made of oak with carved heads, the same length as canes, could also be carried, and were popular from the 1730s. Sticks and canes could have a ring attachment and appended to a coat button or looped to a finger for carrying.

Fob *pocket watches* were carried in the breeches' waistband pocket and the watch case was often made of tortoiseshell or precious metals. The watch had short ribbons through the ring handle where a seal might also be attached. The other end of the key chain and ribbon was usually attached to the waistband itself.

The use of snuff became fashionable at the beginning of the century, so *snuff boxes* were carried in waistcoat pockets. They were made in diverse materials such as precious metals, tortoiseshell, ivory, mother-of-pearl, etc. The lid inside could be mirrored and the outside could be a painted miniature portrait.

The dandies of this century, the Macaronis, spent a great from perfumes and other make-up, they used a small comb for their eyebrows. Face patches were also popular, being fashionable as well as fulfilling the function of covering up blemishes in an age in which skin disease was not uncommon. A lotion, not water, was used for shaving, then rouge was used as a skin foundation. Lavender water was a popular fragrance used as a scent. To enhance the shape of their legs, gentleman used false calves which were made with pads and bandages.

Female Costume

Women's attire consisted of an ensemble: petticoat, and a bodice and skirt joined, called a gown. The skirt was often open in front to disclose the petticoat, which was not worn as an undergarment, but rather as part of the dress, an ornamentation. Separate bodices and skirts were also worn, although mainly by the working class. The bodice was then like a jacket and was worn over the skirt. Gown bodices varied only slightly in the first three-quarters of the century, the sleeves generally being short. If striped materials were used they were used horizontally, except when long sleeves became fashionable, then the stripes could be worn also vertically. Necklines were invariably low.

The skirt shape fluctuated, being dependant on the under structure. A bustle was worn until *c*.1710, and then again from about 1775, but the hoop was popular from 1710 until the bustle again was worn. However hoops were still worn for Court wear until the 1820s.

The *gown* consisted of two types – the *open robe*, which was open in front revealing a petticoat was popular throughout the century; and also the *closed robe* style which was not open in front, and therefore did not require a petticoat. Another style was the bodice and skirt worn separately.

OPEN ROBE 1700–50

The open robe always had a bodice, invariably open, joined to the open skirt. The *bodice*, long waisted until about 1710, was boned and close fitting with the front left open. The openings were edged with sewn-down revers which were known as 'robings' which came from the back of the neck

Jacket and petticoat dress with a domed hoop, c.1718–20

Gown with trained overskirt and a fontange headdress, c. 1700

Open robe with pannier-type hoops. Corset laced in front with quilted petticoat, c.1744

and fell over the shoulders and down towards the centre at waist level where they usually ended. Apart from Court wear these were usually plain before 1745, and not embroidered. The opening in the front of the bodice could be covered in a variety of ways: a stomacher, corset or under-bodice. A stomacher was a stiffened or padded panel with the upper part straight across, making a low square neckline with the robings either side. The lower edge of the stomacher could be either pointed or rounded as well as scalloped. It could also be very ornate with either decorative embroidery or 'echelles' which consisted of a series of bows from top to bottom with the size of the bows decreasing towards the waist. These stomachers were usually attached to the bodice by means of pinning to tabs under the robings. Plain stomachers were more often attached by lacing across and could be covered by a large neckerchief which fell to the waist in the front and was secured by ribbon bands which crossed to the robings on either side, or by a breast knot. The corset type fill-in was similar to a stomacher and could be plain or embroidered and was laced under the bodice at the back.

An *under-bodice*, which was less popular, was without sleeves, unboned and worn like a stomacher, but laced behind.

In the 1720s the bodice could be closed and the décolletage rounded. There were no robings, and closure was in the front with buttoning to the waist. The overskirt was attached to the bodice all the way round and was open in an inverted 'V' shape. *Bodice sleeves*, often weighted near the elbows with some lead from about 1710, were short, ending just below or above the elbows. Until the 1750s sleeves could be gathered or pleated at the shoulders. From about 1700 to mid-century sleeves could have cuffs which were quite small and close fitting. The sleeves could be gathered at the shoulder.

From 1740 *cuffs* became larger and winged, being stiffened to stand out at the outer side and becoming narrower towards the bend of the elbow to allow for freer movement. The sleeve opening was wide enough to allow the chemise sleeve to emerge with its lace-edged frills. From about 1750 sleeves were close-fitting, ending in one or more flounces which were wider on the outer edge and narrower towards the bend of the elbow. As these sleeves were too tight for the chemise frills to emerge, the flounces or ruffles were sewn in separately. The lace edging on the ruffles often matched the lace on head and neckwear. The upper ruffles were always shorter than the lower ones to allow the lace to be visible.

In the very early part of the century the *overskirt* was pleated to the bodice at the back, becoming smooth at the front, ending at the robings, to allow the petticoat to be shown. The overskirt was trained and often looped up over a bustle.

After *c*.1710 hoops were worn, either dome-shaped (until the 1780s) or oval (from about 1713 until the 1740s) after which they became extremely wide (1760s).

The *overskirt*, pleated to the bodice had the back cut 'en fourreau' from *c*. 1730. This meant that the back of the tight-fitting bodice had panels either side of the central seam which converged towards the waist and continued, in one without a join, to expand down the skirt to the hemline. This style of cutting the back was typical of the century and was later known as 'corsage en fourreau'.

With oblong hoops, or panniers, *skirts* were cut in a slightly

(Right)
Street scene. News-sheet seller, c. 1767. The lady on the right is in an open robe with the trained overskirt hitched up, laced stomacher with a crossed handkerchief at the bosom. Straw hat is worn. The man has a coat with round cuffs, waistcoat buttoned to the hem and bag wig à la pigeon. The news-seller has mob undercap, crossed handkerchief at the bosom and a cross-laced corset.

33

different way. The skirt was pleated to the bodice from the robings in the front and from the fourreau at the back to the sides, from whence it continued at the sides in a horizontal seam so that the skirt could hang evenly to the ground over the hoop which stood out on either side. Pleating continued on the horizontal seams which were partially open from the waist forming placket (pocket) apertures through which pockets, if worn, could be reached.

From about 1710 to mid-century *petticoats* were only flounced for Court wear, but were often elaborately embroidered in a different colour to the gown. If worn over a dome-shaped hoop the petticoat was pleated on to a waistband which could be tied at the back, but the more usual way was for ties to be either side forming vents for the placket holes. When the pannier was worn the petticoat, front and back were often sewn to the waistband without pleats and tied at the sides leaving placket holes for the pockets to be reached.

The *mantua*, a variation of the open robe, was worn until the 1750s. It was worn with a petticoat, the bodice unboned and the skirt trained. Although a loose gown, it was richly embroidered and worn on special occasions with a buckled belt or girdle and the trained skirt pinned up.

CLOSED ROBE 1700–50

There were several styles of closed robes which were later known as round gowns. A popular style, known as a *wrapping gown*, was worn until the 1750s. The bodice was close-fitting without robings and a rounded neckline which ended with either a tucker or modesty piece. The front of the bodice crossed over like a wrap and was in one with the skirt. If the wrap-over was not very deep, the front could be fastened with either a clasp or brooch. A girdle could also be worn. The sleeves could have loose cuffs or several ruffles. This type of gown could be worn with all different types of hoop shapes.

When the gown had edge-to-edge closure, as was popular from the 1730s to 1740s, the bodice was similar to that of the wrapping gown with a modesty piece and occasionally a handkerchief. Closure was by means of a brooch or hooks-and-eyes. The back of the bodice was joined to the skirt as a 'corsage en fourreau' with extra pleats at the back to give more fullness. The skirt front had a short fall pleated on to a waistband which tied at the back beneath the bodice which, when

Wrapping gown worn with a pannier, and double ruffle cuffs, c.1740–50

Sack dress, often called the Watteau gown, c.1730

fastened, hid the placket holes at the sides. The sleeves were generally short, cuffed or scalloped.

Another type of closed robe was the *sack* which came to England from France about 1720. The earlier style was very loose-fitting and rather shapeless. The back had box pleats sewn down at the neckline and allowed to flow loosely, whilst the front had the pleats from the shoulders with the front meeting at the waist and filled in with a stomacher or corset. The later style had the bodice close-fitting at the sides with robings which could end at the waist or lower. The sack back had several box pleats each side of the centre seam, sewn down from the neck to shoulder level, and then allowed to hang freely. Hoops of any shape could be worn beneath these dresses.

BODICE AND SKIRT 1700–50

A separate bodice and skirt could also be worn. The bodice was a kind of jacket, tight fitting to the waist and then flared out either to hip level or lower. It was fastened either with laces or by hooks-and-eyes which were covered by a fly. The elbow-length sleeves had cuffs which could be winged.

Another type of bodice, known as the *pet-en-l'air*, worn about mid-century, was a jacket bodice rather like the sack but reaching to about thigh length, or occasionally longer. It was worn with robings and a stomacher. The skirts worn with these types of bodices were worn mainly over dome shaped hoops and sometimes also over panniers. This kind of outfit was worn mainly for morning or informal wear.

(Right)
Lady in open robe style with a handkerchief, and gentleman with large bag wig, c.1770.

In the second part of the century clothes remained basically the same as in the previous half.

The sack style went out of fashion in the 1780s, but was worn as an open robe from mid-century. The bodice, open from that date, could be worn with a stomacher or false front or even a waistcoat from 1770. From about 1760 robings usually reached the ground instead of ending at the waist. They could also be trimmed or embroidered.

In the decade from 1750 the décolletage was very widespread, so that the stomacher, framed either side by the robing, was very broad.

From about 1770 the bodice was closed edge to edge with hooks or lacing, but was without robings. The bodice was still laced at the back to give a close fit, as the back was still loose. The sleeves, which were close fitting to the elbows, could have several flounces, deeper at the back. From about 1770 winged or round cuffs were worn with small frills above and below.

The overskirt, which was similar in style to that of the first half of the eighteenth century, was often worn hitched up, with the corners of the front pulled up, thus forming bunches at the back. Overskirts became trained in the 1760s after which they again became shorter. Petticoats, which followed the lengths of the overskirts, became decorated with flounces.

There were variations in the sack dress, one being known as the *Brunswick* with its short robings and false bodice front and buttoning, and long tight-fitting sleeves. It was an outfit particularly favoured for travelling as it was relatively comfortable.

Another, the *Trollopee* (only worn on informal occasions) was loose with an unboned bodice, trained overskirt, but a short petticoat. As it was worn mainly indoors, an accompanying hoop was not essential.

Also worn until about the 1780s was the *robe à l'anglaise*, a gown with a fourreau back. The bodice, similar to that worn with the sack, could be open with robings and a buttoned stomacher front. If worn without robings, a false waistcoat or *zone* was worn. The bodice was closed at the décolletage and opened in an inverted 'V' to the waist. This gap, the opposite shape to that covered by a stomacher, was filled in with a zone which could be scallop-edged or vandyked. A falling collar edged in matching vandyking which came to the tip of the triangle at the bosom could also be worn.

(Right)
The lady on the left is wearing a wide-skirted dress with an echelle stomacher, and the gentleman beside her is wearing a tricorne hat. The lady in the centre is in a sack dress of silk, worn over a pannier-hooped petticoat. The gentleman wearing the full-skirted pleated coat with deep cuffs has a full-bottomed wig, c.1745–50.

Back of 'pet en l'air' jacket bodice, skirt worn over a pannier, c.1778

The short polonaise worn over a calf-length skirt, c.1778. The ultra-fashionable wig styles were built up high on cushions or pads which were stuffed with horse-hair or wool. The lady here is wearing a 'chignon' which hung at the nape of the neck was often plaited and could be either allowed to hang down the back or looped up on itself and tied into the wig. Accessories were varied from feathers, ribbons, flower displays or large fancy caps (as illustrated) with ribbon lappets or hanging pieces.

A plain, closed bodice was also worn which closed down the front with edge-to-edge fastenings and was without robings, ending at the waist either straight or with a rounded point. The fourreau back, with the bodice and skirt cut in one, fitted at the waistline with sewn-down pleats converging to the waist and then allowed to hang loosely. This 'corsage en fourreau' had a stiffened bodice with strips of cane sewn into the seams.

Sleeves were in varying lengths with either flounces or cuffs, and elbow length until the 1780s when three-quarter length sleeves ended in ruffles. If they were wrist length they had wrist frills. The petticoat for the robe a l'anglaise was in varying lengths to match the overskirt and could be worn with any type of hoop.

A *nightgown* or *negligée*, not worn as night apparel, was an informal open robe with robings and stomacher. It was unboned and made of a fine material and often worn with a white apron with the décolletage filled in. As it was mainly worn indoors a hoop was not necessary. The *Italian nightgown* or robe, popular in the 1770s, was more fashionable than the negligée, and the bodice, without robings, had edge-to-edge closing and ended in a point in the front. The back, made in four parts, was tight fitting and stiffened with whalebones in the seams. The sleeves were usually long with round cuffs. The overskirt was joined to the bodice in pleats, but the front was left open. The train at the back could be hitched up either by fastening the bottom points with a button-and-loop at hip level or with a drawstring which passed through loops inside the skirt near the hem and was drawn up when required. The petticoat was usually in a contrasting colour to that of the gown, but could be decorated or fringed in the same colour as the robe. Aprons could also be worn with this style.

The *polonaise* was extremely fashionable from about 1770–90. A short polonaise (more popularly) had the over-skirt hitched up into three draperies, thus exposing the petti-coat all the way round with the central drape at the back hanging lower than the side ones. The drapes could be formed by threading a cord through loops and pulled up, or with button-and-loop fastening, or else ribbon ties with stitching separating the drapes and hidden by bows. The bodice, with-out robings, could have a low square décolletage or be round necked, either fastening at the bosom and worn with a waist-coat or, if the opening was not too large, filled in with a zone. The bodice could also be closed with edge-to-edge fastening with buttons, lacings or hooks. Sleeves could be elbow length with cuffs, and perhaps a frill, or three-quarter length with several frills. If they were long, the sleeves were tight-fitting with wrist buttons and a small cuff. Petticoats worn with the short polonaise were usually ankle length. If the polonaise was long, as was popular from about 1780–85, the overskirt was usually trained. As fashionable accessories, aprons as well as sashes could be worn.

Back view of caraco dress sometimes worn with a girdle, c.1780

(Left)
The lady on the left is in an open gown with a stiffened corset bodice and padded bustle. The lady in the centre is also wearing an open gown with a matching petticoat dress worn over a padded bustle. The gentleman is wearing a frock coat with the sloped cut and a high stand-fall collar and centre closure, c.1775–85.

The *open robe*, worn from about 1780–94, usually had a close-fitting bodice with the waist line higher than before and the skirt long and full, being pushed out at the back by a bustle. Vandyke edging was very popular and was used on the falling collars and edges. The bodice (with very low décolletage) was often filled in with a 'buffon', a large transparent neckerchief, and decorated with ribbon knots as could the point at the back. The bodice was worn without robings and was fastened in a variety of ways diverging open to the waist. The opening was covered by either a zone or waistcoat. Sleeves were similar to those of the polonaise, either being long, tight fitting and buttoned at the wrists and with small frills, or three-quarter length with either small cuffs or frills. The higher waist was often enclosed by a wide sash or girdle with a jewelled buckle.

Although bustles were usual under petticoats, small hoops could also be worn until the 1780s. The open robe was worn in several variations, with the bodice back en fourreau or with a long train. Different coloured sleeves could also be worn.

CLOSED ROBE 1750–1800

In the 1780s the *closed robe* fashion began to appear again. The fourreau gown was made with the bodice closed in the front by lacing with the skirt pleated on to a band.

The *chemise gown*, very fashionable from about 1783, was made of a fine material, with close-fitting bodice and low round décolletage. The skirt was long and full, and at the waist a long sash was worn which was tied at the back with the ends hanging. The gown could be closed, in which case it was put on over the head. Another style was closed with buttons or ribbon bows all the way down. Sleeves, which were long and tight-fitting, were also buttoned at the wrists. A falling collar which could be vandyked was quite usual.

From about 1785 a riding-coat dress, also worn as a walking dress, was made in a similar manner to the chemise gown, but in a sturdier material. The falling collar ended in revers, similar to a man's coat and the low décolletage was always filled in with a buffon, or by some other means. Buttoning was from the top to the hem line, with occasionally a few buttons left undone at the base to reveal the petticoat. The placket holes in the skirt often had vertical flaps. With this type of dress a sash was not always worn. Another variation of this riding dress had the bodice only buttoned, so that the overskirt, left open, revealed the petticoat, which was

*Tabbed bodice and skirt,
closed-gown style, c.1775*

*Lady in large hat and closed
gown, c.1780*

generally in white. This style was in the open robe fashion.

BODICE AND SKIRT 1750–1800

For informal wear the bodice and skirt could be separated. The bodice, jacket-like and low necked was of varying lengths, sometimes as low as the hips. Fastening was down the front with hooks-and-eyes or lacing. If left partially open a waistcoat was also worn. A style with a sack back, known as the *pet en l'air* had sleeves which were long and tight-fitting with round cuffs with ruffles. The petticoat was often trimmed with a deep flounce and the hoops were usually oblong or dome-shaped.

A thigh length jacket worn in the 1780s was known as the *caraco* and was close-fitting, flaring out from the waist, but without a waist seam and often with a sash or girdle around the waist.

Another type of jacket, known as the *juste*, was worn at the same period as either a morning gown or for riding; close fitting, it had flared skirts joined at the waistline. Sometimes the back could be longer or the skirts could be made in tabs. The décolletage was low and ended with a falling collar. The bodice could either be closed at the front with hooks, or laced over a stomacher. Matching these jackets, the base of the petticoats were often edged or flounced to match the edgings.

ROUND GOWN

From about 1794 most dresses were high waisted, the large bustle having gradually diminished, as did also the buffon filling, giving the silhouette a longer look, with the trained skirts becoming longer. Aprons were less popular and placket holes through which pockets could be reached also became more unfashionable with the advent of handbags.

The *classical style* of open robe had a short bodice with a wrap-over front and could have a rolled collar known as a 'capuchin'. The wrap-over at the waist was hidden by either sash or belt, and the back was so cut that the sleeves were joined to the bodice so far back that a narrow line was achieved. The overskirt joined to the bodice and was trained, was open in the front in an inverted V-shape, revealing the matching, but untrained, petticoat. Sleeves could either be long and close fitting or short and puffed, as well as three-quarter length.

Another fashion was a low-necked bodice which could be either laced or pinned, worn over a round gown or closed

High-waisted fashion with lady carrying an 'indispensable' or handbag, c. 1799

45

robe. The overskirt, in a contrasting colour to the skirt, was trained and only covered the back. The sleeves were usually so arranged that the sleeves of the gown beneath were revealed. The bodice of the round gown worn over this dress was usually high necked so as to appear above the low décolletage of the overgown. The collar could be standing, flat, a small standing ruff or V-shaped. The front of the skirt was gathered on to a band which was tied at the waist behind, whilst the back of the skirt was trained. To prevent the front from slipping, the ties were often looped through loops under the arms first.

Over the round gown could be worn, as an accessory, an overbodice, low-necked and short-sleeved and reaching the thighs. It could be tied at the waist by a ribbon belt. The sides of the sleeves and the bodice could, instead of being stitched, be left open and fastened by ribbon ties.

Another style, which could be worn over the round gown and also over the overbodice if desired, was a short-sleeved basked bodice made like a corset with front lacing and known as a *vest*.

RIDING COSTUME

A riding costume which could also be worn for travelling consisted of a jacket, waistcoat and petticoat. The jacket, similar to a man's frock, being high-necked at first, had a flat turned-down collar. As the jacket became more open the collar was stepped in front to form lapels. Occasionally the jacket was double-breasted, and the skirts curved back more, forming short tails behind. Towards the end of the century the waist became higher and a sash was also worn. The long close-fitting sleeves were buttoned at the wrists. Military-style decoration became very popular from the 1770s in the form of braid edgings and loops and frogs for fastening. The waistcoat was also similar to the man's, being buttoned in the front, left over right. Skirts became increasingly shorter and were cut away from the centre front, sometimes forming rounded points. Eventually, by about 1780, the skirts were no longer there and the fronts curved to a short point. Lapels became so large that they overlapped those of the jacket. The petticoat sometimes had vertical pocket flaps, and was long and slightly trained. Very often the waistcoat was in a different colour and cloth to the rest of the habit which was of cloth. This style of riding habit was the forerunner of the tailored ladies suits of the next century.

Long to-the-ground mantle with hood, c.1745

The lady on the left is in a riding habit made of a woollen cloth. The long skirt had to be carried over the arm. Note the stepped collar. In the centre is seen a milkmaid selling her wares in the street and wearing the older style of costume with a large apron. The gentleman is wearing the silk cut-away coat and square-cut waistcoat, c. 1795

46

The riding habit was constructed similar to men's attire, the coat and jacket cut like a man's with a back vent and pleated side vents. Until about 1765 it was without a collar after which a small turned-down collar, similar to a man's frock was worn. Both the collar and cuffs were faced in a contrasting colour which could be repeated in the waistcoat (usually just a false front with lining at the back). In contrast to men's coats, those of ladies could have the front skirts of the jacket joined by a seam at the waist to form a flare, so that it fitted better over the long, full skirt. Fastening was by means of buttons, left over right, as the men's. Pockets could be set at any angle. Sleeves were long and tight-fitting ending in closed cuffs. A cravat or steinkirk, similar to the male style could also be worn.

OUTDOOR WEAR 1700–50

For outdoor wear *cloaks* were the most popular. Until about 1730 a mantle was worn which was a tent-like cloak reaching the ground. It had slits for the arms, and sported a flat collar. Fastening was by means of buttoning down the front. After 1730 a *mantlet* became fashionable. This was a shortened version of the mantle and was a kind of shoulder cape.

A *tippet*, popular throughout the era, was of fur, made like a cape with hanging ends at the front. A muff in fur to match was often worn as well. Occasionally tippets could also be made of feathers.

OUTDOOR WEAR 1750–1800

For outdoor wear cloaks were still in general use, mostly they were long, ending above the hem of the dresses. The collar could be either flat or with a cape-like hood.

From about 1780 onwards a large long scarf worn around the shoulders, the end hanging down the front, and sometimes with a high stand up collar was known as the *escharpe cloak*. The *pelisse* was a three-quarter-length cloak, worn from about 1750. This was ample in size, but hung down without being flared, having two slits for the arms to pass through. Closure was by hooks or ties in the front, which was slightly gathered. At the back was a flat collar or hood. Short cloaks could also be worn, and when worn for dress occasions were shaped to the neckline, being gored to give a flared effect. Although they could be worn open, they might also be fastened at the top with ribbon bands.

Riding costume with male-type jacket and waistcoat. Full petticoat skirt and beehive hat worn over a wig, c.1778

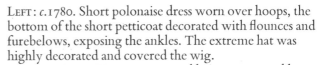

LEFT: *c*.1780. Short polonaise dress worn over hoops, the bottom of the short petticoat decorated with flounces and furebelows, exposing the ankles. The extreme hat was highly decorated and covered the wig.

RIGHT: *c*.1780. Worn over natural hair was a round hat with a flat topped crown and uncocked brim. Single breasted waistcoat worn under a double breasted frock coat. Breeches made of nankeen and short top boots.

Left-hand figure: lady in open gown, threequarter sleeves ending at elbow length with deep frill cuffs. Handkerchief covered the deep décolletage. Short wig hair style. *Man* in single breasted frock with short standfall collar. Centre button fastening, the waistcoat was buttoned from neck line to waist level. Nankeen breeches with silk stockings were worn. Short close-to-the-head wig style. *Boy* is wearing the 'sailor suit' with deep lace collar and wide waist sash. Ribbon bows decorated the trousers at the bottom. Natural hair was worn long. *Lady* on right is wearing the closed gown with the deep bodice and sleeve to elbow length, with short plain cuffs. Deep bertha collar covers the low neck line. The skirt is draped up towards the back, revealing the under petticoat. A full powdered wig with ringlets was worn. Long-to-elbow gloves were worn.

Pelisse, fur trimmed, c.1786

Open robe with close-to-the-arms sleeves with cross-over handkerchief, c.1792

NECKWEAR 1700–50

There were several kinds of neck coverings. A handkerchief, not a pocket handkerchief, was worn, folded diagonally, draped around the neck, the point to the back and the ends tied in a knot at the front, or attached with ribbon-ties to the stomacher. A handkerchief, made of a fine material such as lawn or gauze and often lace edged, was usually a diagonally cut square, so that each half could be used separately.

The *tucker* and *modesty piece* were very similar to each other. They were both frilled and lace-edged strips attached to the low décolletage; however, the modesty piece, unlike the tucker did not continue up the sides.

Silk zone

UNDERWEAR

Hoops were popular from about 1710–80, but continued to be worn even at Court. They could be dome shaped, this effect being achieved by a series of seven to eight hoops in increasing sizes made of whalebone or cane and sewn into a petticoat made of a stiffish material. Another type was of an oblong shape and called a pannier. The cane or whalebone was placed so that an oval shape was achieved with, at each side, an attachment of half hoops hinged so that they could be folded when required. These cages were attached to a waistband and tied with tapes either side.

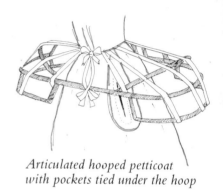

Articulated hooped petticoat with pockets tied under the hoop

NECKWEAR 1750–1800

In the 1750s and 1760s *handkerchiefs* were used as a covering for the low décolletage, the front points being either pinned or tucked into the opening or stomacher and fastened with ribbon bows. In the 1770s when they were larger, they were draped with the ends either left hanging down the front or passed through a ring.

The *buffon*, tucked into the corsage, was a large transparent neckerchief which was bunched up in the front and this, as well as a large shawl-like covering, was popular in the 1790s, draped around the neck, pinned under the chin or worn draped over the shoulders with the ends crossed in front and fastened at the back.

Ruffs were worn throughout from the 1750s. First a small ruff was worn around the neck and could be wired, with the close-set frill around the neck leaving the décolletage bare. Neck frills of high necked gowns were also known as ruffs. The larger ruffs were like capes or falling collars, and consisted of two or three layers of lace pleated on a band falling

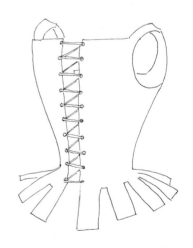

Corset with back and front lacing, c.1768

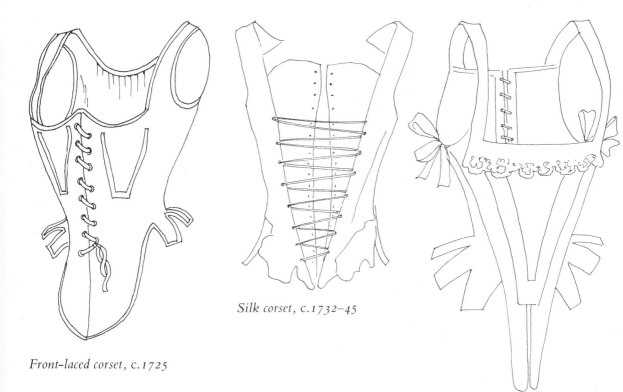

Silk corset, c.1732–45

Front-laced corset, c.1725

Bodice with back lacing, c.1715

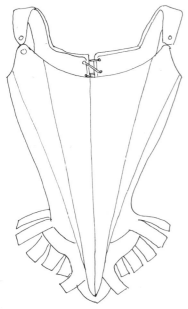

Young girl's whalebone-stiffened corset, c.1730

to the shoulders. The neck edge could also have a small high ruff attached as well.

UNDERWEAR

At the beginning of the century the wearing of the pannier went into decline as a bustle called a *cul* came into fashion. The bustle, enhancing the normal shape in contrast to the unnatural, was made of horse-hair pads fastened to the back at the waist.

In George I's reign (1714–27) *corsets* were made of lavish materials and were worn as bodices. They were stiffened with whalebone with a piece of wire across the top to keep the shape convex. Fragrant herbs and perfume sachets were tucked in the front where there was a concealed pocket. When the corset went out of fashion the bosom was supported by a neckerchief tied either under the chin or around the neck. When the Greek type semi-transparent tunic was in fashion, a *zona* was worn beneath. This consisted of bands worn around the body supporting the lower part of the

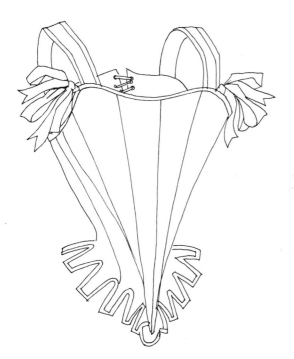

Boned under-bodice worn for
warmth and embroidered, c.1710

Heavily boned silk bodice,
c.1735–50

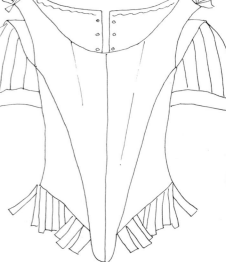

bosom. Shoulder straps were occasionally added to the zona,
making it resemble a corset and elastic, covered in a material,
instead of whalebones was used as support. Waists were
accentuated and the skirts were held out by layers of petticoats instead of panniers. Detachable day sleeves which were
washable, were worn up to the elbow level over more ornate
sleeves. The use of over-sleeves has remained in use for nurses
up to this day.

FOOTWEAR 1700–50

Shoes from the beginning of the century until the 1730s were
pointed with large, waisted heels from 5–8 cm high. The tops
covered the foot with high tongues either square, pointed or
scallop shaped and were fastened with buckles or tied over
the instep. After *c*.1730 the toe-section became shorter and
less pointed, and with daintier heels. Tongues also became
shorter and were more rounded.

Back-laced corset with ribbon
loops, c.1715

Satin shoe with Italian heel

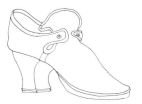

Silk brocade usually tied
with ribbon ties, c.1700–30

Damask shoe, c.1730–50

Shoe made of fine leather,
c.1770–80

Early type of slip-on
slipper, c.1700–30

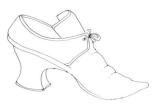

Silk damask shoe,
c.1730–50

FOOTWEAR 1750–1800

A small type of wedge heel was introduced *c.*1753 when buckles were still very ornamental and heavily jewelled.

In the 1750s and 1760s toes were pointed with the heels placed further forward. The tongues became smaller and more rounded with squarish buckles in baroque designs. Toes became more pointed in the 1770s with the heels coloured. The Italian heel was placed forward and was slender waisted. French heels were similar, but higher and the buckles worn with these heels, known as *Artois*, were large and oblong, but were often replaced by other decorations such as rosettes or fringed borders.

In *c.*1786 a low-cut Chinese-type slipper (called a *kampskatcha*) became popular for a short period. Its toes were turned up and the heels small and low. They were often fastened with a running string encased in a ribbon binding at the edge and could be trimmed with a ruching at the front.

Half boots, similar to men's, and shorter ones with rounded toes and low heels were popular from the 1770s for driving and riding. They were fastened in the front by laces.

With the pointed toes for fashionable ladies (*c.*1790), high *Louis heels* were also worn. This heel took its name from Louis XIV and was made in such a way that the sole of the shoe continued up under the arch and down the front of the heel. Ribbon rosettes replaced the previously popular buckles as decoration. Elaborate embroidery was another form of adornment in common use. Many of the shoes were made of a matching material to the dresses, fabric now being popular. Very fashionable was silk and satin, with occasionally ribbon panels forming the vamp.

In the 1790s flat shoes similar to slippers, had small curved wedge-shaped heels. They were low-fronted with short vamps which were sometimes tied with ribbon bows. The toes could be pointed or tip-tilted.

By the end of the century the older fashion of high heels and buckles returned, but soon laces replaced the buckles.

The revival of classical clothes (1790–1804) made the fashion of Greek-influenced flat sandals with criss-crossing up the legs a popular style.

Stockings and flesh-coloured tights were an important part of clothing, especially when the dresses were semi-transparent. Both men and women wore stockings clocked to knee height. These clocks gave more fit and shape to the stockings which were often worn with flat slippers (which

*Satin-embroidered shoe
with high French heel,
c.1755–70*

*8. Silk damask patten,
1730–50*

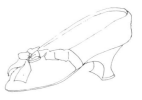

*Damask shoe with ribbon
decoration, c.1770–80*

*Silk shoe with Italian type
of heel, c.1775*

*Silk damask shoe with
wooden heel, c. 1700–30*

Shoe in kid leather, c. 1796

Silk shoe, c.1730–50

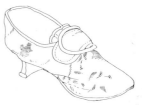

*Satin brocade shoe,
c.1775–85*

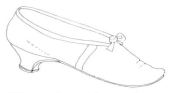

*Slipper shoe with turned-up
toe, Oriental style, c.1786*

*Shoe worn with a clog,
c.1740*

looked like modern ballet shoes or dancing pumps). These
slippers were made of a delicate kid leather, low cut with
various decorations, and very often without heels. (Pattens
resembling mules were often worn with these slippers. They
had low-covered wedge heels over which the slipper heel
sometimes hung. They were secured by a lace bow in front.)
Overshoes known as *clogs* had leather soles and were worn
over shoes. Fashionable clogs were made to match the shoes
with which they were worn. *Pattens* were a type of overshoe
with wooden soles raised on iron rings. The leather tops were
tied with ribbons to secure them to the shoes. As these were
worn mainly for protection on dirty roads, they were mainly
worn by country people.

Stockings were worn to above knee length and were knitted
in thread, cottons or silks of various colours. *Garters* were
lengths of either silk or inkle and had designs or motifs woven
in. They fastened either above or below the knees. In the
1780s shoes, like slippers or mules with low heels, were sometimes fastened with *laces* across the toes.

HEADWEAR 1700–50
The *fontange* (a white linen cap worn at the back of the head
with layers of lace-edged pleats, one above the other) and
supported by a wire frame known as a 'commode', and two
streamers or lappets, hanging either side, was very fashion-

Round-eared cap, c.1745

Round-eared cap with short lappets, c.1736

able until the end of Queen Anne's reign (1702–14), when a lower and less ornate hairstyle became popular with the majority of women, although backcombing and the frizzing remained popular.

All types of caps worn by all classes were to be seen after the fontange had become unfashionable and until the 1760s. There were many styles with various variations. However, the main body of the cap was usually of a white lawn or lace, with trimmings also sometimes of lace. These caps were for indoor and outdoor wear, and frequently worn under hats. At the beginning of the century a cap variation called a *pinner* (small and round), had, instead of the fontange front, a small frill only. The pinner was worn flat on top of the head with a single or double frill and trimmed with ribbon and lace and for further decoration a small bunch of flowers could be attached. If lappets were worn, they hung down behind or were pinned to the crown of the cap.

Another variation had, instead of a frill all round the cap, one at the front only with often a V-shaped dip in the front. The back was left plain, but lappets or streamers could hang behind.

Another popular style for important occasions had a larger frill at the sides which was wired and starched. Other variations had the lappets tied at the front under the chin, or the wired fronts placed heart-shaped and tilted slightly forward. The famous *mob cap* had a full, puffed-out crown with a ribbon tied in the front with several loops. The frill around the cap sometimes had lappets (short or long) at the sides were allowed to hang down or pinned up or tied under the chin. The ties were known as 'kissing strings' or bridles. A wide ribbon encircled the crown. The *round-eared cap* (popular until the 1760s) or coif was bonnet-shaped curving to ear level with the front edged in lace. The back was usually plain and tightened with a running string to fit the head. The hair at the back was often visible beneath the coif. If lappets were worn they were usually pinned up or loosely tied under the chin. It was made of fine material and usually lined in contrasting silk. After *c.*1745 this cap became wider at the sides and was sometimes wired so as to stand away. Lappets became less popular.

HEADWEAR 1750–1800

The *Pulteney cap*, worn in the 1760s, though more favoured by older women, was similar to the round-eared cap, but had wings which stood in two crescent shapes above the forehead with a dip centre front with, occasionally, two short lappets hanging down the back. This cap was often worn with a triangular kerchief with the point behind, over the cap, and the ends fastened under the chin.

After the 1760s the popularity of caps went into decline, getting smaller until only a small square or triangular piece of material was placed over the head, with the point at the back and the two ends tied under the chin or at the back. This was known as the *Ranelagh mob*.

During the 1770s when hairstyles were at their extreme height, the caps worn on informal occasions grew large to fit over these extravagant coiffures, whilst those worn on formal occasions were small and set on the top of the hair. By the late 1780s the mob cap had become enormous and was made of a fine material such as muslin, with soft frills and ribbon bands; after *c.*1790 mob caps tended to revert to their earlier smaller size. Another cap called a *dormeuse* was a French type of nightcap. This was at its biggest and most popular during the 1770s, being worn mainly from 1750–90. It had a loose crown trimmed with ribbons and a bow in front. Pleated or gathered–lace edged the cap mainly at the sides by the cheeks.

High crowned dormeuse, c.1782

Large mob cap, c.1788

These side wings were known as 'cheek wrappers'. Another interpretation of the dormeuse was gable shaped with masses of frilling and lace ruffles, fastening under the chin with a bow. This style later became quite small and was placed on top of the hair.

Caps were also popular in the 1760s made of a length of fine material and draped in a *turban* shape.

The *butterfly cap* worn, mainly at Court, in the 1750s and 1760s was a small cap shaped like a butterfly and made of lace, ornamented with jewels and flowers. It was worn towards the front above the forehead and gave the impression of a butterfly with extended wings.

HATS 1700–50

Straw hats became very popular (after about 1725) due to the expansion of the straw plait industry. A fine wheat straw from Italy (in fact) was used to make the well-known leg-horn plait which was used in the making of straw hats. 'Chip' which was strips of willow or poplar was an alternative material used in the making of plaits for straw hats and was in common use throughout the eighteenth century and into the beginning of the nineteenth century. The *bergère* (shepherdess) type was a low crowned, wide brimmed hat worn previously by country women, and was now worn by all classes. It was fastened by ribbons under the chin, which were attached either side of the crown and over the brim. Sometimes the brim could be turned up front and back, in which case the fastening came from under the brim.

Day caps were usually worn under hats except riding hats which now were of a three-cornered style and worn with a wig. These *riding hats*, becoming smaller towards the end of the century, were made of beaver or felt, with a button and loop trimming on the left side; feathers were also sometimes used as fringed decoration. *Jockey caps* made of black velvet or silk could also be worn, and were also worn with wigs or had hair-pieces attached.

Bonnets came into fashion which were made of 'chip' and decorated with 'blond' (a kind of lace) and feathers or silk trimmings.

HATS 1750–1800

With the elaborate hairstyles of the 1770s hats varied from being enormous to accommodate the coiffure, or small and perched on top. Large hats were ornamented with bows and

Bergère straw hat worn over a mob under-cap, c.1751

wide ribbons, which could be tied in the front above the brim, or allowed to hang down loosely at the back. The brims were often turned up at the back. In the 1780s, when many hats were large, they were worn at all angles and made of a firm material such as felt or straw which was sometimes covered in some other fabric. During the 1780s the *picture style* hat worn with a sideways or, occasionally, a back tilt, became very fashionable. This was a small crowned hat with a large brim ornamented with wide ribbon bands and large feathers.

In the late 1780s tall, crowned hats known as bonnets were worn. These had tall round crowns, flat on top with a slanting brim. The tops of the crowns could be decorated with either feathers or bows and flowers. Very often veils could also be worn with this type of hat, or lace arranged around the brim.

Large, soft hats were also popular during this period and were at first known as *Lunardi* or balloon hats. The full puffed crowns made of silk or gauze were supported by a stiffening on the inside. The brims could either be made of 'chip' or were wired to keep their shape.

Large hat with soft crown, c. 1790

Large hat with a soft crown and a stiff brim, c.1786

Fashionable hairstyle decorated with ribbons, feathers, jewels and a small turban.

Another popular hat shape (from *c.* 1779–81) was the *beehive* which was fitted over tall coiffures.

Hats were worn at a variety of angles. In the early 1780s they were worn at a forward tilt over the forehead, and after *c.*1783, either flat on the head or sideways as well as at a backward slant. The foreward tilted hats with low crowns, soft brims and sloping sides were invariably covered with decorations. Those hats worn flat on the head often had the brims larger at the sides and back, with feathers stuck in the hatband in front. Hats with stiff brims and worn flat on the head usually had the brims decorated with lace all round.

A popular style (a type of bicorne) from the late 1770s to 1790s was with the brim turned up or 'cocked' on either one or both sides and fastened to the crown with either a ribbon rosette, cockade, or button loop.

Another popular riding hat style was high crowned with a flat brim decorated with a hatband and buckle or ribbon trimming.

A jockey cap for riding in the 1750–60s was round crowned with a peak in front, and was always in black. These became unfashionable as hairstyles became more elaborate. In the 1780s a low-crowned round hat with a rolled-up brim and decorative hatband was worn at a slight forward angle.

HOODS 1700–50

Hoods were worn mainly for out-of-doors and remained in vogue until the 1760s, after which they were mainly worn by the lower classes. Fairly large to cover both the hair and caps, they were made of various materials such as velvets and satins, which could be quilted, or gauze. Those in a finer material could be lace trimmed or have ruching. The hoods were either gathered or pleated at the back and some had side lappets which could be tied under the chin or crossed under the chin and tied behind (these hoods were known as the *long hood*). The *short hood* was similar, but tied in front under the chin, and was mainly in black. *Black hoods* were popular and were often lined in contrasting colours; although these were worn for mourning other colours were also used which meant the hood could be worn on a variety of occasions.

HOODS 1750–1800

Hoods could also be attached to shoulder capes, and others – *capuchins* – had deeper capes which were very popular with all classes.

Another type of hood, the *calash*, made its appearance in the 1770s and 1780s. This was a tall construction made of a lightweight material which covered a cane or wire frame and could be folded back when not in use. The front edge could be trimmed with lace frilling and usually tied at the front with a bow under the chin. Large hoods without supports were often attached to capes, whilst the calash was always worn without a cape.

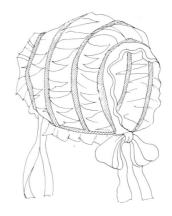

The 'calash' hood made of light-weight material over a cane or wire frame, c.1775

HAIRSTYLES 1700–50

The built-up hairstyles of Queen Anne's reign were replaced by more simple fashions with the hair being combed back and a bun worn towards the top of the head, with occasional curls being allowed around the face, or hanging loosely at the back. A style known as the *Dutch hairstyle* became popular from *c*.1730 and consisted of hair in loose waves, combed back from the forehead with a centre parting and ringlets or curls hanging down the back of the neck. It was particularly popular for formal occasions with pearls or ribbon knots entwined in the hair. No caps were worn with it. Another popular fashion at this same period (1730–early 1750s), was one known as *tête de mouton* ('sheep's head') which was a style of close curls, sometimes with false hair added, and decorations of top-knots which were large bows worn on top of the head, ribbon bunches, artificial flowers, jewels and ornamental pins. Pom-poms worn towards the front or side of the head were an extremely popular accessory throughout the middle of the century. The pom-pom included feathers, ostrich tips, lace flowers and butterflies as well as jewels, and these could all be blended in many combinations.

Wigs became less popular as the century progressed, being worn mainly for riding or sometimes at Court. Hair powder in mainly white or grey was still used in the early part of the eighteenth century for special occasions. Grease and tallow was often used to both stiffen or set the hair as well as to afix the powder.

HAIR STYLES 1750–1800

In the 1760s hairstyles once again became more elaborate and false pieces of hair and wool were used to raise the front hair which was dressed in rows of curls horizontally across the forehead. The back hair was raised and placed in a knot on top. Large plumes were worn as ornamentation.

Fashion dolls which were transported from country to

A 'tête de mouton' coiffure,
c.1745

country and were clothed in the latest fashions, also had their hair constructed in the latest modes.

By the 1770s hairstyles reached great heights from 45–90 cm, and were decorated with a great variety of ornamentation. Padded foundations or wire supports were used to give height to build these elaborate fashions. Long rows of curls were worn either side horizontally, front to back, with one or two hanging down. The back hair could be in a 'chignon', which was a roll of hair either real or false. A smooth and flat effect was achieved by looping the back hair up and fastening it with long pins or ribbons. The hair could also be loosely plaited or twisted and looped up the centre back. These elaborate styles took hours to prepare and were powdered and fixed with pomade before the vast quantity of ornamentation was attached. Thus, these arrangements were left for weeks with just an occasional adjustment. At night all that was removed was the surface ornamentation. A large net was worn to cover the hair, and was fastened with strings under the chin. To avoid this uncomfortable method of sleeping, many ladies resorted to wigs in the fashionable styles. But in any case a head-scratcher made of either ivory or metal, and often with a jewelled handle, was a very useful accessory. Hair curling was by means of rollers made of clay around which the strands of hair were wound.

In the 1780s hairstyles had reached the ultimate height of 90 cm and of extravagant ornamentation. Added to the extremely high, frizzed, curled and powdered hair were ornaments of every description, including flower bunches in various containers such as flower baskets or miniature gardens, model ships, blown glass ornaments and, even, plates of fruit and vegetables! After the 1780s these ornate hairstyles became less fashionable and the high oval shapes decreased in height whilst tending to increase in width. The front part of the hair, known as the 'toupée' became more frizzed and wider at the sides covering the ears. This was known as the *hedgehog style* or 'herisson'. Hair powder of all colours was used, but white was still the most popular. A popular style for horse riding was for the long hair at the back to be smoothly combed and turned up into a loop, tied in the middle like a chignon, with a large bow. Other similar styles were known as 'club' or 'catogan'.

Herisson or hedgehog style of
coiffure, c.1770

BEAUTY AIDS

White lead was still used as the chief ingredient for cosmetics, especially face powders which were used by both men and women, and it was the disfiguring effects of smallpox on the face which made face patches to be so popular, as they disguised the pock marks (white lead itself, however, could lead to serious skin diseases). The *mouche*, as it was also known, was made of silk, taffetas or Spanish leather, in a variety of shapes and colours, and was popular throughout most of the century, until the decline of smallpox due to the beginning of inoculation in the first half of the following century.

Due to the unhealthy diets, teeth became discoloured and decayed, so false teeth made of porcelain were worn. 'Plumpers' (small cork balls) were used to fill out the hollow cheeks caused by loss of teeth.

Fashionable people, both men and women, also favoured false eyebrows of mouseskin, patches and rouge on the face. Lips were also painted with carmine or lipsticks made of plaster of paris and red dye. Perfume which was used as a deodorant was used in abundance both on the body and clothes (which were difficult to keep clean). Perfumed sachets were often sewn inside linings. Lavender water and lavender soap were both particularly popular, although much perfume was, as it still is, imported from France. About 1724 there was an attempt at making cosmetics safer, but although an Act had been passed to ensure the examination of drugs, most people still chose white lead based cosmetics.

ACCESSORIES

Both gloves and mittens were usually elbow length, mittens having a separate open thumb compartment with the rest of the fingers separate and the back of the hand covered. The back seam and top of the mitten were often embroidered, or the top could be turned down to form a small cuff.

Muffs varied in size, being quite large until about 1710 when they became smaller. Small wrist ruffs worn on either wrist were also popular. From about 1780, when muffs became quite large, they were worn on most occasions. They were made of fur and other warm materials and decorated with ribbons, flowers or embroidery.

Pockets were a separate item, and usually made in pairs, joined by a band and tied around the waist beneath the gown skirts. They were oval-shaped with a slit and were reached through the placket holes in the skirt. In the second half of the

A pair of pockets, c.1774

century when it became impractical for pockets to be worn due to the changing shape of the silhouette, knotting bags (or 'reticules') became fashionable. These handbags were made in several shapes, but were drawn in at the top with a running string and suspended from the wrist.

Fans were very popular, especially amongst the more fashionable ladies who particularly favoured folding ones, whilst *masks* lost their popularity after about 1760. Umbrellas and sticks were also carried.

Jewellery consisted mainly of necklaces, rows of pearls fastened by a diamond clasp being popular, as well as earrings, bracelets, miniatures, lockets and pendants suspended from a chain or stay-hook usually of silver and bejewelled. Rings were not so common.

Jewelled buckles for both girdles and shoes, as well as decorated hairpins were popular. Ribbon neckbands were also covered with jewels. Watches, most fashionable during the 1770s and 1780s, were worn on a watch chain which could also hang a miniature, and these were suspended from a girdle or worn around the neck.

Aprons in varying lengths and colours were worn until the 1790s (but were particularly popular when worn with the 'polonaise' dress). They were gathered at the waist with a running string and tied at the back. Aprons were usually made in a fine material and edged with lace or flounces or were even embroidered.

Gloves were often elbow length, made in a variety of materials including leather. They were often coloured, embroidered, and mainly worn only on dress occasions. For riding, gloves were worn short with the long-sleeved dresses.

Nosegays were common and were worn at the bosom in a 'bosom–bottle' which was a small container with water, and was attached with stay hooks to the front of the dress.

Glossary

Apron	Originally a utilitarian garment for working women, but also worn as an important accessory made of a fine material which could be lace edged, but without a bib.
Artois Buckle	Decorative and very large shoe buckle.
Bag Wig	Powdered wig with the ends tied into a black silk bag.
Banjan	Loose-fitting coat made of Indian cloth, worn on informal occasions, fastening in front with either a clasp or hooks. Close-fitting sleeves.
Bergére Hat	Large straw hat, low crowned and flexible brim.
Bicorne	Hat with brim turned up front and back.
Bodice	Top part of a dress, originating from 'a pair of bodies', a medieval boned corset.
Bosom Bottle	Small glass or metal container filled with water for fresh flowers worn at the décolletage.
Braces	Elastic or bands of material used to hold up the breeches.
Breeches	Leg coverings usually ending just above or below the knees.
Buckled Wig	Wig with tightly rolled curls horizontally arranged around the ears.
Buffon	Gauze or other fine fabric to cover the décolletage, puffed up over the bosom.
Bustle	Half cage made of whalebone worn under a skirt to support the fullness at the back.
Butterfly Cap	Small lace cap wired in a butterfly shape. Decorated with lappets or jewels and flowers for Court wear.
Cadogan	Wig with pigtail tied with a narrow ribbon at the back.
Calash	Folding hood on hoops, worn to protect high headdresses.
Calves, False	Pads worn inside stockings to give the legs more shape.
Camisole	Under-bodice.
Capuchin Collar	Roll collar around a V-shaped neckline.

Caraco	Long waisted jacket, usually ending at hip level, worn as a bodice and with a skirt known as a Caraco dress.
Catogan	Club wig with a flat queue turned up on itself and tied with a black ribbon.
Chapeau Bras	Dress hat, mainly carried under the arm, usually a flat tricorne.
Chemise Gown	Of a thin material and always worn with a sash. Low neckline closed down the front with buttons or ribbon bows. Sleeves were long and tight.
Chignon	Mass of hair at the back arranged in a loop or ringlets to hang down.
Clocks	Embroidered decoration or knitted design on the outside edge of stockings.
Clogs	Wooden soled overshoes.
Cocked Hat	Hat with the brim turned up.
Coif	Small white linen undercap.
Commode	Wire frame to support the fontange headdress.
Contouche	Full, loose gown.
Corsage	Upper or bodice part of dress.
Corset	Undergarment re-inforced with whalebone stays.
Cravat	Neckcloth, the ends tied in front in a knot or bow.
Décolletage	Low neckline of a bodice.
Dettingen Cock	Tricorne with the back semi-circular, cocked vertically to back.
Dormeuse	Day cap with a ruched border, sometimes fastened by a ribbon under the chin and the crown puffed up.
Echelles	Type of stomacher decorated down the front with a ladder of bows increasing in size towards the top.
Fall	Buttoned front flap of breeches.
Fantail Hat	Tricorne with the back semi-circular cocked vertically to appear like a fan.
Fantail Wig	Queue at the back hanging loosely in small curls, fanned out.
Farthingale	Hooped structure to distend a skirt.
Flounce	Deep frill either gathered or pleated as decoration.
Fontange	Headdress with tiers of wired lace-edged ruffles.
Fourreau	Overskirt cut in one piece with over-bodice.
Frock	Coat for informal wear with a turned down collar.
Frog	Ornamental braided loop fastening.
Frontlet	Forehead cloth or band worn around the forehead, covered in a cream to help remove wrinkles.
Gaiters	Ankle covering as well as over the top of the shoes, with a strap under the instep and fastened on the outside with buttons.
Gallowses	Braces.

Garters	Ribbon or cord fastening around the legs to hold up stockings – sometimes buckled.
Gores	Wedge shaped panels joined together to give a fullness without bulkiness.
Greatcoat	A surtout overcoat with a flat collar and smaller collar above.
Hessian Boots	Short calf length riding boots curving to a point in front which was decorated with a tassel, but was lower at the back.
Highlows	Boots reaching the calf, laced in front.
Hoops	Circles of whalebone or cane sewn into an underpetticoat to distend a skirt into various shapes.
Hussar Boots	Boots reaching calf length, slightly higher in front, with the tops sometimes turned over, originally a military style.
Inkle	Type of linen tape.
Italian Nightgown	Semi-formal day dress with low necked boned bodice and elbow length sleeves, joined to an overskirt.
Jackboots	Black leather knee high boots with broad heels.
Jockey Cap	Black velvet peaked cap.
Juste	Close fitting basqued coat worn over a waistcoat.
Kampskatcha Slippers	Chinese style of slipper with pointed toe turned up, and a low heel.
Knee Band	Band fastening the breeches tight at the knee.
Kevenhuller Hat	Large felt tricorne, the front brim high, forming a peak.
Lapel	Turned back upper part of the front of a coat or jacket.
Lappets	Pendants on indoor headwear either hanging at the back or sides.
Macaronis	Young dandies extremely fashionable and considered effeminate by their contemporaries.
Mantua	Loose gown with unboned bodice with an open trained overskirt attached. A decorative petticoat or underskirt was exposed.
Mittens	Usually elbow length with the fingers emerging through an opening, the back decorated, covering them with a flap.
Mob Cap	White indoor cap with a frilled border. Side lappets hung loose or were tied under the chin and known as 'kissing strings'. Plain mob caps could be worn in bed.
Morning Gown	For indoor wear, a long loose gown tied with a sash around the waist.
Mouche	Black patch worn on the face as decoration and also to conceal any blemishes.
Muff	Wide band of fur or other warm material to keep the hands warm, also used as a fashionable accessory.
Mules	Backless slippers.
Negligée	Informal attire.
Night Cap	Skull cap with brim turned up, or a mob cap style worn in

	bed.
Nightgown	Unboned, loose dress worn informally for comfort, but not as night attire.
Open Robe	Gown open from the waist to reveal the petticoat.
Pannier	Whalebone cage worn at the hips to extend the skirts, especially at the sides.
Pattens	Wooden platform soles to keep the shoes raised from the dirty roads.
Pelerine	Short cape covering the shoulders.
Pelisse	Three-quarter length cape or cloak with a hood and slits for the arms to protrude.
Pet-en-l'air	Long jacket with a sack back and short sleeves. Worn with a plain skirt and a stomacher front.
Petticoat	Underskirt which could be highly decorated with flounces, jewellery or embroidery when exposed under the open overskirt.
Physical Wig	The front hair swept back, whilst the back stood out, to below the nape of the neck.
Pinner	1) Hanging streamers of headwear. 2) Type of tucker or 'fill-in' for a low décolletage.
Placket	Slit or opening, usually just below waist level at the sides to allow for access to the pockets.
Plumpers	Small cork balls placed in the hollows of the cheeks to fill them out.
Pockets	Separate items, usually in pairs. Small bags attached to a tape and worn around the waist beneath a skirt, and reached through the placket holes.
Polonaise	Top of boned bodice closed, then cut away to reveal the waistcoat. The skirt draped into three parts held up by draw strings.
Pomatum	Perfumed lubrication for the hair.
Pulteney Cap	Wired under cap with two curves and a dip to the forehead. It could have two lappets behind.
Queue	Hanging tail of a wig.
Ramillies Wig	Wig with long queue of plaited hair tied with a black bow, top and bottom. Sometimes the plait was turned up on itself and secured.
Redingote	Riding coat, double breasted and with a collar or collars and cape. For the ladies, similar to the men's, but open at the waist to reveal a skirt.
Reticule	Small handbag.
Rever	Turned back edge of a coat, waistcoat or jacket.
Robe à L'Anglaise	Sack back gown with the pleats sewn down to waist level.
Robe à la Française	Close fitting bodice with a decorated stomacher, double

	pleats at the back falling loosely from neck to hemline.
Robings	Flat trimming or border around the neck and down the front of a bodice, sometimes also down the edges of an open overskirt.
Roquelaure	Large full cape with cape collars and slit, buttoning down the front and a back vent for horse riding.
Roll-Ups	Long stockings worn over the knees and turned down at the breeches into a roll.
Round-Eared Cap	Head fitting indoor cap, the front border frilled and the back plain and high revealing the hair. Lappets were not unusual.
Round Gown	Dress with a skirt and bodice joined in one, and closed, not exposing the petticoat. The skirt sometimes trained.
Rowel	Spiked wheel attached to spur.
Ruff	Circular collar, starched and goffered sewn on to a band, radiating from the neck.
Ruffle	Strip of material pleated to a straight edge forming a frill.
Sack Back	Box pleats sewn down from neckband to shoulders and then allowed to hang down freely.
Sack Gown	Loose dress, the back pleated to the neckband, and hanging down in folds.
Sash	Band of soft material, the ends tied but not buckled, around the waist.
Scallop	Edging indented with an inverted part-circle shape.
Shawl Collar	Turned-over continuous collar without lapels.
Slit Pocket	Coat pocket cut vertically.
Solitaire	Black ribbon worn over a stock.
Spatterdashes	Leggings reaching over the knees, laced or buckled on the outside. Sometimes extended over the feet with a strap beneath.
Spencer	Short waist length jacket buttoned in the front.
Stay Hook	Small hook attached to the front of a corset or bodice to hang a watch or other items.
Steinkirk	Cravat named after the Battle of Steinkirk, with the ends tucked into a coat buttonhole or into the décolletage, usually lace edged.
Stock	High stiffened neckcloth fastened behind with a buckle.
Stomacher	Inverted triangular stiffened material used as a fill-in for an open bodice. Could be decorated or jewelled.
Surtout	Long loose overcoat usually with cape collar.
Tête de Mouton	False curls over the whole head.
Tippet	Short shoulder cape.
Toupée	Wig with hair brushed straight back.
Train	Base of the back of a skirt, longer at the back.
Tricorne	Three-cornered cocked hat.

Trollopee	Loose unboned morning gown.
Tucker	White frilled edging to a low-necked bodice.
Under-waistcoat	Short sleeveless waistcoat worn beneath a waistcoat.
Vent	Slit, usually vertical from the hem of a garment.
Vest	Undergarment worn for warmth.
Waistcoat	Usually a sleeveless jacket with the front made of a better material than the back, and worn under a frock or coat.
Wig	Artificial hair covering the head.
Zona	Classical-type brassière.
Zone	Fill-in for an open bodice.

Select Bibliography

Arnold, J., *Handbook of Costume*, Macmillan 1973

Asser, Joyce, *Historic Hairdressing*, Pitman 1966

Boehn, M. von, *Modes and Manners* (8 vols), Harrap 1926–35

Barfoot, A., *Everyday Costume in England*, Batsford 1966

Boucher, F., *History of Costume in the West*, Thames & Hudson 1967– *20,000 Years of Fashion*, Abrams

Bradfield, N., *Historical Costumes of England*, Harrap 1958

Brooke, Iris, *History of English Costume*, Methuen 1937; *English Costume of the 18th Century*, A & C Black 1964; *Western European Costume*, Theatre Arts Books 1963

Calthrop, D.C., *English Costume*, A & C Black 1906

Contini, M., *The Fashion from Ancient Egypt to the Present Day*, Hamlyn 1967

Cooke, P.C., *English Costume*, Gallery Press 1968

Courtais, G. de, *Women's Headdress and Hairstyles*, Batsford 1971

Cunnington, C.W., P.E., *Costume in Pictures*, Studio Vista 1964; *Handbook of English Costume in the Eighteenth Century*, Faber & Faber, 1954; *Dictionary of Costume 900–1900*, A & C Black 1970

Davenport, M., *The Book of Costume*, Bonanza 1968

De Antfrasio, Charles & Roger, *History of Hair*, Bonanza 1970

Francoise, Lejeune, *Histoire du Costume*, Editions Delalain

Garland, M., *The Changing Face of Beauty*, Weidenfeld & Nicolson 1957; *History of Fashion*, Orbis 1975

Gorsline, D., *What people wore*, Bonanza

Halls, Z., *Men's Costumes 1580–1750*, H.M.S.O. 1970; *Men's Costumes 1750–1800*, H.M.S.O. 1973; *Women's Costumes 1600–1750*, H.M.S.O. 1969; *Women's Costumes 1750–1800*, H.M.S.O. 1972

Hansen, H., *Costume Cavalcade*, Methuen 1956

Hartnell, N., *Royal Courts of Fashion*, Cassell 1971

Kelly, F.M. & Schwabe, R., *Historic Costume 1490–1790*, Batsford 1929

Kelly, Mary, *On English Costume*, Deane 1934

Koehler, C., *History of Costume*, Constable 1963

Laver, James, *Concise History of Costume*, Thames & Hudson 1963; *Costume*, Batsford 1956; *Costume Through the Ages*, Thames & Hudson 1964

Lister, Margot, *Costume*, Herbert Jenkins 1967

Moore, D., *Fashion Through Fashion Plates 1771–1970*, Ward Lock 1971

Norris, Herbert, *Costume and Fashion*, J.M. Dent 1924

Pistolese & Horstig, *History of Fashions*, Wiley 1970

Rupert, J., *Le Costume*, Flammarion 1930

Saint-Laurent, C., *History of Ladies Underwear*, Michael Joseph 1968

Truman, N., *Historic Costuming*, Pitman 1936

Wilcox, R.T., *Dictionary of Costume*, Batsford 1970; *The Mode in Costume*, Scribner's 1942; *The Mode in Hats and Headdress*, Scribner's 1948

Wilson, E., *History of Shoe Fashions*, Pitman 1969

Yarwood, D., *English Costume from the 2nd Century BC to the Present Day*, Batsford 1975; *Outline of English Costume*, Batsford 1967

Pictorial Encyclopedia of Fashion, Hamlyn 1968

Index